THE
250
ESTATE PLANNING
QUESTIONS
EVERYONE SHOULD ASK

Lita Epstein, M.B.A.

BUSINESS

Avon, Massachusetts

Published by Adams Business
An imprint of Adams Media, an F+W Publications Company
57 Littlefield Street, Avon, MA 02322. U.S.A.
www.adamsmedia.com

ISBN 10: 1-59869-415-4
ISBN 13: 978-1-59869-415-4

Printed in the United States of America.

J I H G F E D C B A

Library of Congress Cataloging-in-Publication Data
is available from the publisher.

This publication is designed to provide accurate and authoritative information with regard to the subject matter covered. It is sold with the understanding that the publisher is not engaged in rendering legal, accounting,
or other professional advice. If legal advice or other expert assistance
is required, the services of a competent professional person should be
sought.
—From a *Declaration of Principles* jointly adopted by a Committee of the
American Bar Association and a Committee of Publishers and Associations

Many of the designations used by manufacturers and sellers to distin-
guish their products are claimed as trademarks. Where those designations
appear in this book and Adams Media was aware of a trademark claim, the
designations have been printed with initial capital letters.

This book is available at quantity discounts for bulk purchases.
For information, call 1-800-289-0963.

CONTENTS

INTRODUCTION

Estate planning involves understanding tax law and being able to manipulate financial equations to figure out how to give away all you've built and accumulated while you are here and after you are gone. You'll find that estate planning has a language of its own, and it's filled with words you've probably never used before or never used in the way they're used here.

I can't promise you that you'll be able to plan your estate after reading this book, but you will have a good idea of key issues to discuss with your accountant and attorney as you put together your estate plan. You won't feel so lost when your attorney tries to determine whether you want a Power of Attorney Trust or a QTIP Trust and whether you want to use a Crummey Trust or a bypass trust to help fund your grandchildren's education.

You probably don't care, as long as your goals are met, but it helps to understand the basics. In this book I start with the essentials of estate planning, talk about the advantages and disadvantages of probate, convince you why it is important to have a will and not die intestate, talk about will substitutes, delve deeply into gift and estate taxes, and discuss types of property transfers that may be necessary to divide your assets.

I also explore how life insurance can help you pay those estate taxes and how you can minimize the amount of taxes your estate will have to pay.

Estate taxes are a moving target, thanks to the ridiculous law that Congress passed called the Economic Growth and Tax Relief Reconciliation Act of 2001. To keep the cost of that law under limits specified by President George W. Bush, the Congress played a dangerous game with estate taxes. The amount of wealth you can exempt from gift and estate taxes gradually goes up until 2010. If you die in 2010, your beneficiaries won't have to pay any taxes on your estate. But that is only for one year. Then the old estate tax law comes back into play.

So what do these shenanigans mean to your pocketbook? In 2007 and 2008, the first $2 million of an estate is excluded from taxes. In 2009, the exclusion amount increases to $3.5 million. Then in 2010, no estate taxes are due. In 2011, if Congress doesn't act fast, estate taxes will be due on any estate worth more than $1 million.

In addition to worrying about estate taxes and how to minimize them, think about what happens if you become incompetent during your lifetime. It's not a pleasant thought, but it's better to plan for it, just in case.

Finally, I present special types of estate planning in which you leave something to someone you lived with but to whom you were not married. People who are not married can't take advantage of many of the laws that married people use to avoid estate and gift taxes.

All of this is critical to help you decide how your assets will be divided after you're gone or maybe while you are still here. The only alternative is to let the government do it for you, something most people don't want to happen.

Chapter 1

THE BASICS OF ESTATE PLANNING

Before getting into the nitty-gritty of estate planning, I want to introduce you to the key terms and concepts you need to understand. This chapter reviews the overall goals of estate planning, who needs to do it, and why.

Question 1. **What is estate planning?**

Estate planning is the process of determining what you want to happen to your estate, which includes all the rights, titles, and interests that you have in the property you own. When preparing a plan, consider the accumulation of that property, how you want to conserve its value, and finally how you want to distribute your estate after your death. Throughout this process, consider the best ways to effectively and efficiently accomplish these tasks, keeping both tax and non-tax objectives in mind.

Estate planning and financial planning have many of the same concerns, including income-tax planning, investment planning, insurance planning, and retirement planning. There are three main objectives of estate planning:

1. Preserve the wealth that has been passed down through previous generations.
2. Use the wealth as desired during your lifetime.
3. Pass on to your heirs the greatest possible amount of that wealth in the appropriate form after your death.

There are several key words that are unique to estate planning. I will present them in greater detail later, but I want to introduce them here.

- Probate is the process of proving who is entitled to get the property if the person who died did not make that clear before his or her death.
- Testator (male) and testatrix (female) refer to people who leave a valid will upon their death.
- Intestacy is what an estate is called if there is no will. Partial intestacy means the will did not effectively dispose of all the assets.

Three types of property classifications are generally used in estate planning:

- Real property includes land and any permanent improvements on that land.
- Tangible personal property includes property other than real estate that has a value because of its physical existence. This includes such things as cars, furniture, and collectibles.
- Intangible personal property includes property that you can't touch but that has a value because of the legal rights you hold. This can include a stock certificate or an installment note but can also include copyrights, patents, and other intellectual property rights.

Question 2. **Who needs estate planning?**

Just about everyone. Even though you may not be wealthy, some degree of planning will probably be necessary.

Here are a few examples:

People with minor children. You need to specify who will care for the children upon the death of their parents and how you will provide for that care financially. You normally make these provisions in your will.

People who own assets in multiple states. Estate planning will avoid what is called *ancillary probate*, in which an additional probate process must be completed in a state different than the one in which you resided because you owned real estate in that second state. Ancillary probate can be very costly and can reduce the value of your estate.

People who own a small business. You must determine what should be done with your interest in that business—whether it is to be passed on to your heirs or sold. If it is to be sold, you must be certain that your interest in the estate will be marketable at the time of your death.

People who will have to pay estate taxes. If your estate is large enough that taxes will need to be paid upon your death, you must plan for that payment. You want to be sure you have enough liquid assets to avoid the forced sale of estate assets. Often this is done with life-insurance planning.

People who want to determine how their assets will be divided among their heirs. If you don't specify how you want to divide your assets, the state will do so as part of probate.

People in high-liability occupations. If you're in an occupation that has a high risk of being sued or facing claims from creditors, estate planning will help protect your assets. Doctors are a prime candidate for this type of planning.

People whose spouses are not U.S. citizens. You will need to provide for your spouse's death. The marital deduction is not available in most cases for a spouse who is not a U.S. citizen.

People who think they may become disabled. You need to appoint a surrogate decision maker as part of your estate planning. Your surrogate will be able to make medical and financial decisions for you. You may also need to plan for possible Medicaid eligibility as part of your estate-planning process.

Question 3. **What are the financial goals of estate planning?**

There are two areas of financial goals: non-tax financial goals and tax-related financial goals. Here, I'll focus on the non-tax goals, which will involve issues such as preserving your business's value, maximizing your estate's financial flexibility, maximizing benefits to your surviving spouse, minimizing non-tax transfer costs, and maintaining adequate liquidity. Your tax-related financial goals will focus on how to minimize your estate's tax bite, including:

- *Preserving your business's value.* Without proper planning, the value of your business could plummet at your death. Maintain the value by using buy-sell agreements among the owners that lay out the distribution of the business upon one of the owner's deaths. Usually these agreements are funded with life insurance policies.
- *Maximizing your estate's flexibility.* The key to keeping an estate's flexibility is to make it as easy as possible for your heirs to access your liquid assets after your death by using certain types of trusts (see Chapter 11), POD (payable on death) designations for bank accounts, and TOD (transfer on death) designations for brokerage accounts.
- *Maximizing benefits for surviving spouse.* The best way to be sure your spouse won't be socked with a lot of taxes upon your death is to place the spouse's estate in a trust that gives

the surviving spouse access to both the income and principal of the trust. Minimizing non-tax transfer costs. Ways of paying as little in fees and costs as possible in your estate planning include will substitutes, such as taking a title to property with joint tenancy with right of survivorship. This will allow you to avoid the costs of setting up a trust.

- *Maintaining adequate liquidity.* You must plan for enough cash and cash-equivalents as part of your estate to cover all the immediate non-tax and tax costs of settling the estate. Cash equivalents can include money market accounts, IRAs, and other investments that can be easily converted to cash. Cash needs after your death are most commonly met with life insurance policies when you put together your estate plan.

Question 4. **What are the non-financial goals of estate planning?**

The non-financial goals focus on several issues: meeting the needs of dependents, properly distributing assets, and controlling your assets after your death. When considering the needs of dependents, the amount of planning will depend on the degree of support the dependent will need. For example, a minor child who can be expected to attain full capabilities when she or he attains adult age will need less planning than a disabled child who will need planning for the basics of life. You will need to specify who will be responsible for a disabled child's clothing, food, and medical care.

Proper distribution of assets involves more than just deciding who gets what. You also must decide the most efficient way to transfer the assets, so the transfer can be done as quickly and orderly as possible.

Another key non-financial goal is control. With a properly drawn will, you can be certain your assets will go to the people you intend to get them.

Question 5. What are the tax goals of estate planning?

These goals will depend on the type of tax involved. Tax goals are grouped into two pots: one for income taxes and the second for transfer taxes, which include gift, estate, and generation-skipping taxes. Tax goals related to income tax involve minimizing taxes through shifting the receipt of income, shifting the taxation of income, and deferring the recognition of income and gain. Tax goals related to the various transfer taxes involve freezing or reducing the value of assets subject to tax; using exclusions, exemptions, deductions, and credits; and delaying the payment of taxes. Chapters 6 to 10 focus on these tax questions.

Chapter **2**

TAKING TIME FOR PROBATE

After your death, any property you own needs to be distributed appropriately. Even if you have left a will, your personal representative will need to complete a process called probate before disposing of your assets. This chapter reviews the basics of probate and the statures that impact the disposition of your assets after death.

Question 6. **What is probate?**

You've probably heard the most difficult process after a person's death is probate. Probate is derived from a Latin word that means "to prove." In probate, you must go before a judge to prove that the will is valid. You must be able to prove several key things:

- The document you present is the will the person intended to be presented as his last will and testament.
- The person whose will you are presenting is dead.
- The will you are presenting has not been revoked.

■ The will was properly executed and was valid in the state in which it was executed.

Each state has its own laws about probate, but in most cases you can prove these things using an affidavit by the person appointed in the will as the deceased person's personal representative. That representative is called an *executor*, if male, or *executrix*, if female.

If the person died without a will or with a will found to be invalid or incomplete, some additional issues must be investigated and established during probate in most states:

■ Was the deceased married and survived by his or her spouse?

■ Was the deceased survived by lineal descendants (which include children, grandchildren, great-grandchildren, and stepchildren)?

■ Were the children also the lineal descendants of the surviving spouse?

■ Does the deceased have lineal descendants who are not the lineal descendants of the surviving spouse?

Question 7. What property interests are affected by probate?

Whether probate after your death will affect property you own depends upon how you took title to that property. If you took title in the form of "joint tenancy with right of survivorship" or "tenancy by the entirety," you've probably designated who the owner of the property should be upon your death, and the property will need to go through probate.

If you took title to the property in the form of "sole" owner, "tenancy in common," or "traditional community property," you will need to designate in your will who should get the property because it becomes part of your probate estate, and it will need to go through the probate process.

Question 8. **What are the objectives and process of probate?**

After a person dies, his assets are distributed in a process called probate. There are three objectives of the probate process:

1. To distribute the property according to the provisions of the will
2. To pay the legitimate claims of creditors
3. To collect taxes on the estate

The process is controlled by a probate judge, whose job is to make sure the three objectives are met. First, the assets of the estate must be pulled together and secured. Then an inventory of the assets is filed with the judge. Creditors must be notified by mail, and a notice must be published in an appropriate public place, such as a newspaper where probate notices are generally published. Any valid debts, expenses, and taxes must be paid before the probate assets can be distributed to the heirs. Once all is done to the satisfaction of the judge, the assets can be distributed.

Each of these steps must be done within time frames set by the court. That ensures the person who has been appointed as a personal representative of the decedent cannot drag her feet and delay the process indefinitely. Also the judge makes sure the property is being disposed of in a trustworthy manner and that the proper records are kept of how the money is used (to pay creditors or taxes) and distributed.

Question 9. **Who is a personal representative, and what are his or her duties?**

When drafting your will, you must designate a personal representative who will carry out your wishes after your death. In most states, this personal representative is called an executor (if male) or executrix (if female). If you die without a will, the state will appoint a personal representative, who can be called an administrator (if male) or an administratix (if female).

If you have appointed a personal representative in your will, the probate court will likely honor your wishes unless it finds a good reason to deny them, such as the court finds your personal representative to be untrustworthy. If you did not appoint a personal representative, or if you die without a will, then the state appoints a personal representative for you based on state statutes. State statues specify a priority list of people who can be appointed as personal representatives. First priority goes to a surviving spouse, then adult children of the deceased, and so on. If the state can't find an appropriate relative, an attorney or bank will be appointed to handle probate.

The key duties of the personal representative include:

- Collect money in bank accounts titled solely in the decedent's name
- Notify all financial institutions that any communications about the decedent's assets should be sent to the personal representative
- Collect any money due to the decedent, such as rents, payments, salary or wages, or life insurance policies.
- Pay any money due to valid creditors of the deceased
- Pay all taxes due
- Manage estate assets during the probate process
- Distribute any estate assets left after the payment of all valid creditors and all taxes

Question 10. **What is a will?**

The primary purpose of a will is to make provisions for how you want to dispose of any property after your death. There are several different types of wills:

- *Simple (or single) will.* This type of will involves a single document with provisions executed by a single maker.

- *Joint will.* This type of will involves a single document with provisions executed by more than one party. It is most commonly used by a husband and wife.
- *Mutual wills.* This type of will involves single or multiple documents executed by two or more parties. The parties contract with each other to leave their property in a specified manner.
- *Reciprocal wills.* This is a type of mutual will in which each party names the other as the recipient of his or her property.

While there are several different types of wills, financial planners exclusively recommend the use of simple wills. All other types of wills can make it impossible for a surviving party to make changes in her or his estate planning after the death of a party to the will.

Question 11. **What is a community property state?**

A community property state gives your spouse an undivided half-interest in all your property, both real estate and personal property acquired during the marriage. The only exception is property acquired by gift or bequest. This interest is given even if the spouse's name is not on the title to the property. The surviving spouse, if not on the title, must assert his or her rights during probate process. States with community property laws include Arizona, Idaho, Louisiana, Nevada, New Mexico, Texas, Washington, and Wisconsin.

Question 12. **What is a common law state?**

In common law states, any property acquired by a married person during marriage is the property of that person separately, unless the person agrees with his or her spouse to hold the property jointly. In common law states, a surviving spouse is given a certain percentage of the property by statute. The common law states may set a flat percentage without regard to the length of the marriage or may set a percentage based on the length of the marriage. In either case, the statues usually declare that a maximum percentage is usually 50 percent of the assets belonging to the deceased spouse can go to his or her survivor. If your state is not listed in Question 11, you live in a common law state.

Question 13. **How do laws differ between a community property state and a common law state?**

When it comes to estate planning and the distribution of assets, the primary difference between the common law and community property states involves the ownership of property and the proportion of that property that must be distributed to the surviving spouse. In a community property state, a spouse has an undivided right to half of the deceased spouse's property even if the property is not titled in the surviving spouse's name but is instead titled to a third party outside the marriage. During probate, the surviving spouse can assert ownership of the property for which she was not on the title. In a common law state, the surviving spouse's portion of ownership is a percentage of the deceased spouse's assets, which can be determined by the court based on the length of the marriage.

Question 14. **What happens if a child is omitted from the will?**

In most states a child who has been omitted from the will can claim a share of the property provided:

- There is no evidence that the omission was intentional.
- The will leaves an amount to the surviving parent that is sufficient to provide for the child.
- The decedent made other provisions for the omitted child outside the will. (Thus, if the child was being taken care of—say, through a trust outside the will—and was omitted

from the remaining estate included in the will, he could claim a share of that remaining property. That fact that something was left to the child helps prove he was not intentionally omitted.)

If you draft a will and want to avoid omitting a child who was not yet born at the time you executed your will, include a clause that includes children born at the time of the will as well as any born afterward. If you want to disinherit a child, state that clearly in the will or your child could file claim for part of your property.

Question 15. **What rights do adopted or illegitimate children have to an estate?**

They have the same inheritance rights as naturally born children in most states. An adopted child does not have the right to inherit from his or her birth parents because the birth parent's rights were terminated when the adoption was allowed.

You are not obligated to leave any property to an adopted or illegitimate child, but if you want to be certain that child does not receive any property after your death, you must state that in your will.

Question 16. **What are abatement statutes?**

If someone is left out of a will and successfully makes a claim during probate, then the court must decide how to split up the assets to provide for the omitted person, whether it's a child or spouse. To avoid holding court hearings each time this situation occurs, states have enacted abatement statutes, which specify the order in which the amount of property to go to each heir will be reduced.

The most common situations in which the portion left to an heir must be reduced are when a spouse claims a statutory share rather than the share that is left to him or her in the will or when, after paying the debtors' claims, expenses, and taxes, there is not enough to pay all heirs the amount specified in the will. You can specify an abatement order in your will, which the state will honor. If you don't specify a priority order, the state abatement statute will be used to determine the order by which shares of your estate will be reduced.

Question 17. **What are ademption statutes?**

Sometimes a person specifies that an asset in the will should be left to a specific person, but at the time of death, the asset is no longer available. Probate courts must determine whether the inheritor deserves a replacement asset from the estate or at least the cash value of the missing asset. The property that is missing is called adeemed, and remedies for adeemed properties are specified in state laws known as ademption statutes.

States deal with this issue very differently, so if you plan to leave a specific asset to someone, check with your attorney about what will happen if that asset is not available at the time of death. If you are supposed to inherit an asset that is no longer available, most states put a heavy burden on you to prove that the deceased intended for you to get a replacement asset if the asset was no longer available.

Question 18. **What are anti-lapse statutes?**

If a person named in your will dies before you or before probate is complete, a probate court must determine what to do with the assets left to that person. How the probate court will handle this situation varies greatly, but unless the will contains instructions on what to do in such a situation, the probate judge will turn to the state's anti-lapse statutes to make a determination. When drafting your will, if you name a contingent beneficiary, you can avoid allowing the probate judge to decide how to split any assets left to a person who died before you.

Question 19. **What are divorce or annulment statutes?**

Suppose you named your spouse in a will and the marriage was annulled or you divorced but did change your will. Can your ex-spouse still inherit the amount you specified in the will? Most states answer no. The statutes that impact what happens to a decedent's property involving a dissolved marriage are called divorce or annulment statutes.

Question 20. **What are simultaneous death statutes?**

In many cases, the disposition of property at the time of death depends on who survived whom. If you are dealing with a life insurance property or financial assets, such as a mutual fund, you probably designated a primary beneficiary or beneficiaries who get the money if still alive and secondary beneficiaries in case the primary ones are dead. Couples often take property as joint tenancy with rights of survivorship or by the entirety, so property automatically passes to the person who survives.

But what happens if both you and your specified heir die simultaneously. Every state has adopted some form of the Uniform Simultaneous Death Act to provide for these situations. As long as your state hasn't changed the language of this act, the basic terms are that each of the parties is presumed to have survived the other. This statute will not be used if it can be determined that one person survived the other, even if only for seconds. Since the act presumes each of the parties survived the other, the provisions of their wills would be followed. For example, suppose you and your spouse died in a car crash and no determination could be made as to who survived longer. Further suppose you each left your share of the estate's assets separately. Under the act, 50 percent of the estate would follow your spouse's provisions, and 50 percent would follow your provisions.

Question 21. **What are tax apportionment statutes?**

When more than one person inherits property from the decedent, sometimes there can be disagreement as to which source should be used for the estate taxes. This can become particularly tricky if one person, such as the spouse, inherits the home and no cash assets while the child or children get cash assets. Where should the cash come from to pay the taxes?

This question is settled by state statutes known as *tax apportionment statutes*. It can be an easy answer if the home transferred to the spouse without generating the need for taxes. In that case, any taxes due would be paid out of the children's share. In some states, the order from which taxes are taken is set by statute. If that is the case, then you can specify the order you prefer, and the state will honor what you have written in your will.

Question 22. **In which state does probate occur?**

Many people spend part of the year in one state and part in another, such as summers in New York and winters in Florida. This can cause some confusion upon death. Where should probate take place: in Florida, in New York, or both? If the person dies without a will, the portion of the estate the spouse would get could be different depending on state laws. Personal property is probated in the decedent's domicile (permanent residence), while real property is probated in the state in which it is located.

For example, suppose a person goes to Florida to avoid winter in New York, but he considers New York his personal residence. Probate would take place in New York, but if he owned real property in Florida, an additional probate proceeding would be needed. The additional probate proceeding would be called *ancillary probate*.

Question 23. **What is the difference between residence and domicile in estate law?**

In probate law, this is an important difference. A residence is the place where the person is staying at the time of death. A domicile is the place the person considers her permanent home and the place she will return to after her visit. The primary probate state will always be the state of domicile. Often both the residence and domicile are the same.

Question 24. **What are the advantages of probate?**

While many people dread the thought of going through the probate process, it does have advantages:

- *It's orderly.* A neutral party, the probate judge, oversees the collection of the assets, development of the inventory, notification of the creditors, payments to creditors and tax collectors, and the disbursement of the assets to the heirs. If the personal representative does not have strong skills in this area, the judge can be essential.
- *It's open to all parties.* Probate can serve as a forum if there are any disputes or critical issues to be decided. Beneficiaries can be certain they will receive inherited property with a valid title. They can also be sure that what they receive cannot be claimed by creditors or by the tax collector. Creditors can be assured of a process for payment of valid claims. Governmental agencies can be certain to get their share in taxes.
- *It's fair.* The probate judge serves as a disinterested, unbiased arbiter of any disputes. The judge can be particularly important if someone questions the validity of the will or the specified distribution of assets.

Question 25. **What are the disadvantages of probate?**

While there are significant advantages to probate, there are disadvantages as well:

- It's costly. When taking an estate through probate, everybody wants a share of the pie. Payments are usually made to an attorney, an accountant, appraisers, auctioneers, and the personal representative.
- It's lengthy. The actual length of time will depend on the complexity of the estate to be settled and that can take years. For example, if a small business is involved and estate taxes are more than can be paid at the time of the death, they can be paid in installments over as long as fifteen years. The estate is opened for that long, and estate assets cannot be distributed until all taxes are paid. To avoid this problem, many small-business owners will take life insurance to pay the anticipated estate taxes.
- It's public. In most cases, your personal estate information is open for public inspection.

Chapter 3

WHEN THERE'S A WILL

I mentioned a will briefly in Chapter 2, but this chapter takes a closer look at what makes a valid will and its key clauses. While you can buy a workbook or computer software to draft your will, your best bet to avoid problems during probate is to seek legal assistance in drafting and executing your will.

Question 26. **What are the requirements for a valid will?**

To be valid, all wills must meet certain basic requirements. These include:

> *Minimum age.* The person writing the will must be of legal age to write a valid will. That age is eighteen or nineteen in most states.

> *Testamentary capacity.* A person who makes a will, a *testator* (if male) or a *testatrix* (if female), must have the testamentary capacity to make the will. This involves three elements:

1. The will maker must understand the nature of the document he or she is signing.
2. The will maker must understand the nature and extent of his or her property.
3. The will maker must understand who is in his or her family— that is, the will maker must understand who is a family member and who is not.

The term *of sound mind and body* captures the most important elements of testamentary capacity.

Valid form. The will must be in a form that is recognized as valid in the state in which it will be executed. Every state authorizes a typewritten or witnessed will, but some people like to be more creative. If you want to use another form for your will, be sure it will be recognized as valid in your state.

Property executed. Every state has requirements about how the will should be executed. Be sure you know the requirements for your state, and follow them exactly.

Question 27. What are the typical clauses of a will?

Common wills are broken down in to four types of clauses: preliminary clauses, dispositive clauses, appointment clauses, and concluding clauses.

1. *Preliminary clauses* set the stage for the will with identifying information including the name of the maker, the maker's domicile, the fact that this is meant to be the maker's will and the revocation of any prior wills.
2. *Dispositive clauses* specify who should get the assets.
3. *Appointment clauses* specify the personal representative and his or her fiduciary responsibilities, as well as any guardianships.
4. *Concluding clauses* seal the validity of the will, including signatures of the maker and required witnesses.

Question 28. **What are dispositive clauses of a will?**

The dispositive clauses are the core of the will, where the maker specifies how his assets will be distributed. Since the will is often written long before the death of a person and the actual property that will be owned at the time of death may be different than that owned at the time the will was written, specific property items are seldom mentioned unless they are family heirlooms or other assets that will definitely be there at the time of death.

These clauses should be written directly with a clear command of how the property should be distributed. If the words *wish* or *hope* are included, the court may decide not to honor those wishes or hopes. Real property is disposed by a *devise* and the recipient is known as the *devisee*. Personal property is disposed as a *bequest* or *legacy* and the recipient is a *legatee*. If the assets to be disposed are specifically named, then it's a *specific bequest*. If the bequest is to be paid out of the general assets, then it's a *general bequest*.

If you have many small items to list in the will that are not of great value, include a *tangible personal property clause* that will list the items and to whom they should go. Some states allow people to include a document that is separate from the will called a *tangible personal property memorandum* to dispose of small items. The advantage of the memorandum is that since it is not part of the will, if you want to change it, you don't have to go to the expense of executing a new will.

In some cases, you may not want to give the asset directly to the beneficiary but instead transfer the property to a testamentary trust. The will should also include terms for how the trust must be distributed. If the trust already exists and will be added to at the time of your death, then it's known as a *pour-over trust*, and the will is a *pour-over will*. I talk more about trusts in Chapter 5.

In all cases, the will should name both a primary beneficiary (first priority) and contingent beneficiary (who gets the assets if the primary beneficiary is not alive) for each asset named in the will. This will avoid any problems if a beneficiary dies before you do.

Question 29. What are appointment clauses of a will?

The most important appointment clause in any will is the clause that specifies the personal representative. Question 9 explained who the personal representative is and briefly described his or her duties.

In addition to appointing a personal representative to administer your will, you also may need to appoint guardians. For example, if you have children, you should specify who you want to be the guardian and conservator of your minor children. Some people may also specify a guardian and conservator for favorite pets.

You may also want to include a fiduciary powers clause that specifies the powers you want to give your appointees. If you don't include this clause, your appointees will only be able to do what is specified by state statute.

Question 30. What are concluding clauses of a will?

The first of the concluding clauses reaffirms that the document is your last will and testament and includes your signature and the date that you signed it. That clause is followed by the attestation (statement of witnesses) clause. The witnesses affirm that they saw you sign the will and that you had testamentary capacity at the time of signing (that is, you were "of sound mind and body"). This clause should include all the essential statements that the witnesses would have to verify if they were called to personally testify at the time of probate. If so, this can also serve as a self-proving clause, which means that the proof that the will is valid can be assumed and the courts won't need to talk with the witnesses.

Both your signature and the signatures of the witnesses must be notarized. If your state does allow the attestation clause to be admitted to probate court without personal testimony, be sure that your concluding clauses are done in the form specified by state statute.

Question 31. **What is a no-contest clause in a will?**

If you want to leave someone out of your will, be sure to include a no-contest clause. This type of clause usually specifies that if you want to disinherit a family member but that family member successfully challenges the provision in your will that disinherits him or her, then the family member receives only a nominal amount that you specify, such as one dollar. This clause can also state that if a beneficiary contests the inheritance because he or she is not happy with the amount received, then that amount is revoked and distributed as if that beneficiary had died before the testator or testatrix.

Probate judges may not enforce a no-contest clause because it takes away the right of a family member to exercise his right to legally contest the will. Some states have statutes regarding how no-contest laws should be treated by the probate court.

Question 32. **What are other common clauses in a will that are optional?**

Other common clauses specify disposition of assets or payment of taxes. If you anticipate that there will be estate taxes, you may want to include a clause specifying how those taxes should be paid. If you have intangible property, such as a copyright or patent, you may want to include an intangible personal property clause to specify who will control those rights. If you have many different parcels of real estate, you may want to include a real-property clause to specify the disposition of the property. To be sure all property is disposed of, even if not specifically named in the will, you may want to include a residuary clause that disposes of all probate property not effectively disposed of in other clauses of your will.

Question 33. **How do you amend or revoke a will?**

All wills are totally revocable until your death. Each state has its own laws specifying how you can amend or revoke a will. If you want to change your will, be sure to follow the rules of your state to avoid any problems during probate.

If you want to revoke a will, your best bet to ensure it is never used is to collect all the copies and destroy them. If that is not possible, keep the original and write the word *revoked* on the front of it. The word *revoked* should be handwritten by the maker.

If you want to revoke a will, be sure you have already executed a new will before you write *revoked* on the old will. If you don't do this and you die before the new will is completed, the court will consider that you died intestate (without a will), and the state will determine how your assets should be distributed.

Chapter 4

INTESTATE—WHEN THERE'S NOT A WILL

If you want to have some control of what happens to your assets, you don't want to die intestate—without a will. This chapter explains what happens to your assets if you die without a will.

Question 34. What happens if you die without a will (intestate)?

Some people can't even sit down and think about their death, so they never prepare a will. Others prepare a will, but it does not dispose of all assets effectively. If a person dies without a valid will, he or she is said to die "intestate," and the state laws of intestate succession take over. Each state has its own set of laws to deal with intestate succession, and the probate proceedings are called intestacy proceedings.

Sometimes a person will die in partial intestacy, with only some of his assets not properly disposed of in a will. Avoid this by including a *residuary clause*, which specifies the disposition of leftover assets.

A person who has no valid will and has property not held in a will substitute form, such as property titled joint tenancy with right of survivorship, is said to die in total intestacy. When this happens, the state laws determine what goes to whom, and the state appoints a personal representative for the deceased. (Question 9 covers the duties of the personal representative.)

Question 35. In intestacy laws, what provisions are made for survivors?

Surviving family members have first priority. The states believe that the decedent's spouse and lineal descendents (children, grandchildren, great-grandchildren, adopted children, and illegitimate children) should get most of the property of the deceased. Before the state will even consider the rights of more remote family members, the spouse and lineal descendents must be cared for appropriately. The proportion of the estate that goes to the eligible family members is specified by state law.

Question 36. What provisions can be made for charities or non–family members?

Most states have no provisions for charities or non–family members. That's because the state has no way to know which friends and charities the deceased would want to give part of the estate. Even if a charity or friend could prove there would have been something left had the decedent made a will, there is no way for the state to know how much.

This can be a very difficult situation if the couple were not married and lived as domestic partners. Some states have amended their statutes to include a "registered domestic partner" in their intestacy statutes, whether the partner is of the same sex or of the opposite sex. If your state allows you to register as a domestic partner and the relationship is dissolved, be sure to officially terminate the record with the government. If not, your registered domestic partner may have the right to claim assets from your estate if you die intestate and if the state provides for domestic partners in their intestacy statutes.

If you want money to go to a charity or non–family member, make a valid will with that information included.

Question 37. **What provisions are made if there are no surviving family members?**

Sometimes a person dies with no will and no surviving family members. All states include statutes that specify what to do if there are unknown heirs. The state will hold the decedent's property in trust for a number of years, as stated by law. If no one comes forward to claim the estate within the specified time, the property belongs to the state. This property is said to escheat to the state.

How closely related do you need to be to make a claim on the estate? Each state specifies the degree of kinship required to make a claim.

Question 38. **How is the estate distributed if a person dies intestate?**

After the payment of all claims by creditors and any taxes due, the estate will start distribution of the assets by giving the spouse his or her share as stated in the intestacy statute. This could be the entire estate if there are no lineal descendants. In some states, the spouse may get all the assets even if there are surviving lineal descendants, if these descendants are also the descendants of the surviving spouse. Each state has its own laws, so if you want to have some control over the distribution of your assets, you must make a valid will.

Question 39. **What are the disadvantages of intestacy?**

There are many disadvantages of intestacy. The only advantage is that you don't have to deal with what happens after you die.

Here are some important disadvantages:

- Intestacy laws as written in each state must be applied rigidly. There are no provisions for special needs. For example, if you have a disabled child and want to set aside a larger share for his or her care, the state laws won't allow for that special circumstance if you die intestate.
- The share each heir gets is set by law, so the assets will not be distributed based on what you think is best for each heir.
- All children are treated equally, regardless of age or competency.
- If you have minor children, a guardian or conservator will be appointed by the court, and it may be someone you would not have wanted to be in charge of your offspring.
- Most states have no provisions for domestic partners or other nonfamily members.
- No state has provisions to give part of your estate to charity.
- Estate taxes could be higher because the property will be distributed by state law, and that distribution may not minimize the tax bite.
- The state will name your personal representative, who will administer the disposition of your assets.

Don't die intestate. Take the time to prepare a valid will, so you can be sure your assets will be disposed of in the way that you want.

Chapter 5

WILL SUBSTITUTES, OR HOW TO AVOID PROBATE

Probate can be a long and complex process. You can make it easier for your heirs by using will substitutes to avoid or minimize the need for probate. Most of your major assets can be passed on using will substitutes. This chapter reviews the key will substitutes you can use.

Question 40. **How can you avoid probate?**

Luckily every state offers some ways to avoid probate for major assets, so your family doesn't have to wait for the probate process to be completed to make use of or dispose of those assets after your death. Since probate can take a year or more, this can be a huge benefit when you are dealing with a home or other key assets.

When property is involved, you can own that property with a title that names the survivor's rights. These types of titles automatically transfer the property to the joint owner, when one of the owners dies.

Another common way to avoid probate is to name a beneficiary when you purchase the asset or insurance policy. This type of will substitute is commonly used to avoid probate when people open accounts with banks, brokerage houses, or mutual funds or when they buy an insurance policy.

Question 41. **What are rights of survivorship?**

Two types of property titles offer the right of survivorship. The most commonly used are joint tenancy with the right of survivorship (JTWROS) and tenancy by the entirety (TBE). The first type, JTWROS, means all owners of the property own an equal and undivided share of the property. When one of the owners dies, the property ownership automatically transfers to all other owners. This type of ownership does avoid probate but can be a problem when the last surviving owner dies. At that time, the property needs to go through probate.

Only a married couple can use TBE. Neither spouse can sell or take a loan on the property without the other spouse's permission. After the death of one spouse, the property automatically transfers to the surviving spouse; there is no probate. The property will have to go through probate after the death of the sole surviving spouse.

Question 42. **What is joint tenancy?**

Any time two or more people share ownership in real-estate property or other assets such as a bank account, when one owner dies, that property can transfer automatically to the surviving owners without the need for a will or probate. For example, if you open a bank account with your child as joint tenants, your child can automatically become full owner without the need for a designation in your will.

There are actually three types of joint bank accounts:

1. *Joint tenancy with immediate vesting.* Each owner has an immediate right to half the account but cannot withdraw more without letting the other owner know.
2. *Revocable account.* Either owner can withdraw all the funds in the account without seeking permission of the other, so neither owner's interest is vested.
3. *Convenience account.* One person deposits all the money, and a second person serves as an agent for managing the funds. The person who deposited the money has sole rights to the funds. This type of account is typically used by a child who is assisting an elderly, incapacitated parent.

Question 43. **What is a beneficiary?**

A beneficiary is any person or organization that has the legal right to receive assets or other benefits through a legal document, such as a will, trust, or insurance policy. Many types of will substitutes can be used to designate a beneficiary and avoid probate:

- Government savings bonds
- Payable-on-death (POD) accounts
- Bank account trusts or Totten trusts
- Transfer-on-death (TOD) accounts
- Contract provisions in pensions, IRAs, annuities, and life insurance policies.
- Gifts causa mortis
- Revocable living trusts
- Irrevocable living trusts

Questions 44 to 50 cover how each of these types of will substitutes can be used to avoid probate.

Question 44. **How can a government savings bond be used as a will substitute?**

To use a government savings bond as a will substitute, you'll need to buy Series EE bonds. You can buy these bonds using a right of survivorship designation or a beneficiary designation. If you choose a right of survivorship designation, then you and someone else are buying the bonds as co-owners, and the surviving owner gets the proceeds upon the death of the other owner without having to go through probate. If you choose a beneficiary designation, you control the bonds completely and can change the beneficiary at any time before your death. Upon your death, your beneficiary would get the proceeds without having to go through probate.

If you have property to leave, you can't use bonds as a will substitute. You can use bonds as long as you name a beneficiary or buy them with right of survivorship. For example, a father and son buy bonds with right of survivorship. When the father dies, the son gets full possession of the bonds without having to go through probate. Or a husband and wife buy bonds and name their children as beneficiaries. The children can get the bonds when their parents die without have to go through probate.

Question 45. **How can POD accounts be used as a will substitute?**

When you open a payable-on-death account, you maintain complete control of those funds while you are still alive. Any assets left in that account after your death are then transferred to your designated beneficiary without the need for a will or probate. Beneficiaries are usually spouses, children, or a charitable organization.

Question 46. **What are Totten trusts?**

If you want to use this type of trust, you deposit money in a bank account for the benefit of another person but maintain control of the money until your death. Prior to your death, you have the right to withdraw funds at any time. Your beneficiary can't touch the money while you are still alive. This is also known as a revocable trust using a bank account. Only thirty-six states allow this type of trust, so check with your financial adviser or attorney to find out if this is even an option in your state. After your death, the trust transfers to the beneficiary without a will or probate.

Even if this trust is available in your state, you may not want to go through the expense of setting it up. You can have the same control with a POD account and avoid the hassle and expense of establishing the trust.

Question 47. **What are TOD accounts?**

Transfer-on-death accounts operate in a similar fashion to POD accounts. The primary difference is that TOD accounts are used for publicly traded securities and debt obligations. While the registered owner is alive, he maintains total control over the securities in the account. After he dies, the securities transfer to the designated payee without a will or probate. The beneficiary designation is revocable, so the owner of the TOD can change the designee at any time while he's alive.

Question 48. **What are gifts causa mortis?**

In a few states, you can make a revocable gift called a gift causa mortis if you believe you are near death. Your death must be imminent for this will substitute to be used, but it can reduce gift taxes. Causa mortis is Latin for "contemplation of death." A gift causa mortis is both conditional and revocable. If you survive the illness or other peril that you thought would result in your death, the gift is automatically revoked. You can revoke the gift at any time for any reason if you are alive.

This type of will substitute is rarely used as an estate-planning tool. Most attorneys will recommend a trust or other formal arrangement if you wish to designate a gift after your death.

Question 49. **What are revocable living trusts?**

All states recognize the use of revocable living trusts. With this type of trust, you transfer assets to someone but keep the power to revoke the trust at any time. You must fund this type of trust before you die to avoid probate.

You can draw up the trust agreement to transfer the assets upon your death to a designated beneficiary, or you can designate a later time for the assets to transfer to your beneficiaries. All assets in a revocable trust can be transferred to the designated beneficiaries without a will or probate, as long as you don't revoke the trust prior to your death.

Question 50. **What are irrevocable living trusts?**

An irrevocable living trust has almost all the same characteristics of a revocable living trust discussed in Question 49. The primary difference is that the person who grants the trust to someone cannot change his or her mind later. The beneficiaries of the trust have a vested interest in the trust, and that interest cannot be revoked.

Question 51. **How can provisions in contracts be used to avoid a will?**

Every time you fill out the forms at your workplace for life insurance or employer-sponsored retirement plans, you are signing a contract that likely has provisions to avoid the need for a will or probate. When you designate a beneficiary as part of those forms, you are essentially completing a will substitute. The assets in your retirement account or the proceeds from the life insurance policy will transfer to your designated beneficiaries automatically without probate. Any life insurance policy, individual retirement account, annuity, or other type of contract you sign designating a beneficiary works the same way as employer plans after your death.

Question 52. **What are the advantages of a will substitute?**

The biggest advantage of any will substitute is that it will help your heirs avoid the expensive costs and delays of having to go through probate. You can also transfer your assets privately without having to file them with the probate court.

Many will substitutes are revocable, so you maintain control over the disposition of those assets while you are still alive. This can also be a disadvantage because revocable assets are used as part of the owner's gross estate and are taxable at death.

Question 53. **What are the disadvantages of a will substitute?**

The biggest disadvantage is that you must fund the substitute prior to your death—that is, you must put in the assets you intend to include. This can be a big factor if you are funding a trust, POD, or TOD. Will substitutes can be costly, especially if you want to set up a revocable or irrevocable living trust. You must hire an attorney to establish the trust initially, and you may need to pay maintenance fees as assets in the trust are purchased or sold. You will also need to file tax returns if you set up an irrevocable living trust.

Chapter **6**

DEALING WITH TAXES— FEDERAL UNIFIED TRANSFER TAX SYSTEM

Estate taxes or "death taxes," as they are frequently called, are in a state of flux and will be until the U.S. Congress determines what it will do after 2010. In 2007 and 2008, the first $2 million of an estate is excluded from taxes. In 2009, the exclusion amount will increase to $3.5 million. Then in 2010, the estate tax will be repealed—if you die that year, your family won't have to pay estate taxes. But, if Congress doesn't act to extend that repeal of the estate tax law, in 2011 estate taxes could go back to excluding just the first $1 million in assets. This chapter explains the law as currently written, but be aware that will likely change in 2011. This makes it difficult to do long-term estate planning.

Question 54. **What is the federal unified transfer tax system?**

The federal unified transfer tax system combined the gift taxes (taxes on gifts made during your lifetime) and estate taxes (taxes on your assets passed on at your death) in 1976. Prior to that time, the two types of taxes were separate. Today, the same tax rates are used to determine both your estate and gift tax liability. With this system, a $250,000 taxable gift would be taxed in the same way as a $250,000 taxable estate provided there had not been taxable transfers prior to your death. The maximum gift or estate tax rate for 2007 to 2009 is 45 percent for gifts or estate exceeding the maximum exclusions.

With the passage of the Economic Growth and Tax Relief Reconciliation Act of 2001, the gift tax maximum exclusion from taxation is $1 million, and the maximum exclusion for estate taxes is $2 million. Anything you leave to your spouse is entirely excluded from gift or estate taxes, provided your spouse is a U.S. citizen. This tax system also makes possible for you to transfer your assets by a lifetime gift or a bequest at death to a qualified charity and reduce the tax liability of the estate.

The amount of your estate is cumulative, and both gifts and transfers of property after your death are totaled to calculate the full value of your estate under the unified system.

Question 55. **What is a gift tax?**

A gift tax is a tax due on gifts over $1 million during your life-time. You can avoid ever having to pay a gift tax provided you give $12,000 or less to an individual each year. A couple can give up to $24,000 because the law treats the gift as though one-half of the gift was given by each spouse. These limits can be adjusted by the government annually for inflation. Provided you don't give more than $24,000 in any one year, all the gifts could be given without using up any of your $1 million gift tax exclusion.

You can also give away an unlimited amount of money provided the gift goes directly to an educational institution for tuition. So you can pay the tuitions of all your grandchildren without having to worry about gift taxes. You can also avoid gift taxes if you pay a medical provider for any uninsured medical expenses for a third party. For example, suppose wealthy grandparents want to fund cancer treatments for a grandchild, and the amount will exceed $12,000. As long as they pay the cancer treatment center directly, the money given will not be included in gift tax calculations.

Question 56. **What is an estate tax?**

An estate tax is a tax on your estate after your death. When you die, any property or assets that you leave behind are part of that estate. The federal government taxes that estate before the assets can be transferred to your heirs. How much that tax will be depends on the size of the estate and when you die. In 2007 and 2008, the first $2 million of an estate are excluded from taxes. In 2009, the exclusion amount will increase to $3.5 million. Then in 2010, no estate taxes will be due. In 2011, if Congress doesn't act fast, estate taxes will be due on any estate worth more than $1 million. Tax rates would range from 41 percent on estates over $1 million to as high as 60 percent on estates between $10,000,000 and $17,184,000. Estates over $17,184,000 would be taxed at a rate of 55 percent.

Question 57. **What is a generation-skipping tax?**

The federal government doesn't want to miss collecting taxes during each generation, so if you try to avoid taxes by giving your estate to your grandchildren rather than to your children, you might have to pay a generation-skipping tax. For example, suppose you decide to give a sizable gift of $1 million to your grandchild. You would have to pay both the gift taxes and the generation-skipping taxes on that gift. You can avoid paying any gift taxes by applying that gift to your applicable credit amount of $1 million in gift taxes. You can still skip generations by giving money to your great-grandchildren or great-great-grandchildren, or any person who is more than one generation younger than you, because a gift tax is only applied once even if you skip more than one generation with your gift. You won't be subject to generation-skipping taxes if you pay medical or educational expenses directly for any of person who is more than one generation younger than you.

Question 58. What is EGTRRA, and how does it impact the federal unified transfer tax system?

The Economic Growth and Tax Relief Reconciliation Act of 2001 (EGTRRA) created a temporary change to the gift and estate tax system that expires in 2011. Congress wanted to keep the tax cut to a certain size, and repealing the gift and estate tax completely would have been too expensive. So instead they passed this nightmare that leaves everyone guessing as to what will happen to gift and estate taxes in the future. It's very hard to plan an estate, when you have no idea what the tax will be on that estate in 2011. If Congress does not act, then the estate and gift taxes will revert to what they were before the passage of EGTRRA, which means just $1 million will be excluded from gift and estate taxes. Tax rates would range from 41 percent on estates over $1 million to as high as 60 percent on estates between $10 million and $17,184,000. States over $17,184,000 would be taxed at a rate of 55 percent. (See Question 56 for further discussion of this.)

Question 59. What is the marital deduction?

If you're married, the marital deduction allows you to offset or reduce your estate from tax liability by transferring it to your spouse. You also get a gift tax marital deduction to offset any gift tax liability when you give your spouse a gift. Essentially anything you give as a gift to your spouse or leave to your spouse in your estate will not be taxed thanks to the marital deduction.

Question 60. **What is the charitable deduction?**

You can reduce your tax liability with a gift to a charitable institution using the charitable deduction. Any gift or bequest to a charitable institution will reduce the taxable amount of your estate. For example, suppose you die in 2009, when $3.5 million is excluded from estate taxes and your estate totals $4 million. You can avoid estate taxes completely by donating $500,000 to charity. (See Chapter 8 for how to use charitable donations in estate planning.)

Question 61. **What is the applicable credit (or unified credit)?**

The applicable credit (formerly known as the unified credit) allows you to exclude a certain amount of your taxable transfer from the calculation of estate tax. This credit is part of the Internal Revenue tax code. The amount of your estate that will be free from taxes is determined by Congress. Question 58 explains the current state of estate law.

Question 62. **What is the fair market value of an estate?**

The key to figuring out how much your estate is worth depends on the value established for the assets you are transferring either as a gift or after your death. The U.S. Treasury Department defines fair market value (FMV) as "the price at which property would change hands between a willing buyer and a willing seller, neither being under a compulsion to buy or sell and both having reasonable knowledge of the relevant facts. The fair market value of a particular item of property includible in the decedent's gross estate is not to be determined by a forced sale price. Nor is the fair market value of an item of property to be determined by the sale price of the item in a market other than that in which such item is most commonly sold to the public, taking into account the location of the item wherever appropriate."

The IRS will question certain types of property transfer. For example, the price an employee pays for property from an employer could be questioned, so if you plan to sell your business to an employee to avoid estate taxes, expect some scrutiny from the IRS regarding its value. Also a forced sale situation, such as an auction, cannot be used to determine the fair market value. The price the IRS will use to determine value is the retail value of the property. Questions 63 to 72 present more specifics of fair market value based on the type of asset involved.

Question 63. **How do you determine the fair market value of real estate?**

This can be a difficult task because there are so many factors that are relevant to the calculation. The key elements to setting a fair value for a parcel of real estate include:

- Condition of the property, including consideration of its physical qualities and defects
- Size and location of the property
- Actual and potential use of the property with consideration of trends, such as the increase in property value if the land has been rezoned from residential to commercial and is now more valuable as commercial real estate
- Suitability of the property for actual or intended use
- Applicable zoning restrictions
- Size, age, and condition of any structures on the property
- Market value and sales of comparable property in the area
- Value of any net income received from the property
- Probate court valuation
- Cost of making improvements on the property to make it salable
- Uniqueness of the property

Another factor in valuing real estate could be whether the decedent owns the property fully or owns just a partial share of the property. If the real estate is jointly owned and cannot be sold because the surviving co-owner (co-tenant) refuses to sell, the IRS allows a discount to the property's value in the estate. This discount can only be claimed if the co-owners are not related by family (spouses or close relatives) or business associates. Any property owned in joint tenancy with the right of survivorship or tenants by the entirety (see Questions 41 and 42) will not qualify for this discount.

Question 64. How do you determine the fair market value of closely held stock?

If you own stock in a closely held company, such as a family business or a partnership with friends, valuing that stock can be a difficult task. Some key factors include:

- Nature and history of the business
- Outlook for the economy and the industry in which the business operates
- Book value of the stock
- Earning capacity of the company
- Dividends paid annually to the stockholders
- Recent stock sales that show its value
- Fair market value of comparable public stock

You may be able to get a discount on the value of the stock in a closely held company if you are a minority stockholder for estate tax purposes. To qualify for this discount, your minority status must mean that you are not able to influence business decisions or force the business to liquidate, merge, consolidate, or sell.

Question 65. **How do you determine the value of life insurance?**

If the person insured under the insurance policy and the decedent are the same person, the value of the death benefit payable minus any loans or other charges against the policy will be used as the value of the life insurance policy.

But if the decedent bought the policy and the insured is not dead, the calculation of value becomes much more difficult. If the decedent leaves you life insurance on someone who is still alive at the time the decedent dies, then the value of that life insurance is not based on the face value of the policy. In fact, if the payments on the life insurance policy are not made after the decedent's death, the death benefits may never be paid.

Instead the value of life insurance on someone who is not yet dead is based on the replacement value of the policy in question. For example, if the policy was bought just a year before, the value of that bequest would be the premiums that had been paid. If the policy was a single-premium policy or is completely paid up, the value would be based on the issuing charge for the policy based on the age of the insured at the date of transfer.

If a whole life policy is transferred as part of the estate that has a cash value, the terminal reserve (terminal value) plus the unearned portion of the last premium will be used to determine the value unless the surrender value is greater. The surrender value is the cash value of a whole life policy. When you buy a whole life policy, part of the yearly premium is added to a cash account, which grows through the life of the policy. If the surrender value is greater, that value will be used. If a term policy is transferred as part of the estate, the unused portion of the last premium is used to determine value.

Question 66. **How do you determine the fair market value of corporate stocks and bonds?**

When you inherit stocks or bonds that are traded on the public markets, the valuation of these assets can be fairly simple. The fair market value of a stock or bond is calculated by the mean between the highest and lowest stock or bond price on the date of valuation. For example, if the market price of a stock at its high on the date of valuation is $20 and the low was $18, the mean would be $19.

Things are a bit more complicated if the stock was not sold on the date of valuation. Then the fair market value would be the weighted average of the means between the highest and lowest trading dates before and after the valuation date. For example, suppose the stock in question sold for $10 per share for three trading days before the valuation date and $15 per share for two trading days after the valuation date, then the value of the stock would be $12, using this formula from the IRS:

$$\frac{(3 \times 10) + (2 \times 15)}{5 \text{ days}} = 12$$

You can easily get the market value of a public stock in any newspaper that prints information about stock sales or on numerous financial Web sites. For example, Yahoo! Finance (*finance.yahoo.com*) can give you daily historical prices throughout the lifespan of most stocks.

Question 67. **How do you determine the fair market value of annuities?**

Annuities are a type of life insurance product that pays money to individuals or an entity based on some prior deposit of funds by the person or entity who is to receive the payments. For example, people who get a lump-sum payment out of their company 401(k) plan often use this lump-sum payment to buy a single-premium annuity that will guarantee them a set payment for the rest of their lives in retirement. Payouts of the funds can be structured in many different ways.

If you inherit an annuity, the value of this stream of payments must be determined for estate tax purposes. If the annuity is issued by an insurance company, the value of these survivor benefits is determined by the premium charged for the issuance of a single life annuity based on the survivor's life as of the deceased date of death. If the annuity is a private annuity, the value is calculated by determining the present value of the future payments from the annuity or trust. The IRS publishes a *Cumulative Bulletin* that includes actuarial tables for use in determining the present value of an inherited annuity.

Question 68. **How do you determine the value of a U.S. government bond?**

Determining the value of U.S. government bonds can be done fairly easily by getting their redemption price at *www.savingsbonds.gov*. If you don't want to use the Internet, the value of that bond is based on the value as of the transfer or valuation date, which is determined by tables published by the Bureau of Public Debt and the Treasury Department. Most banks can figure out the value using those tables.

There are currently five types of savings bonds on the market: Series E, H, I, EE, and HH. Series E, H, and HH bonds are no longer issued, but many have still not reached maturity and are still held by investors. Series EE bonds have been on the market since January 1, 1980. Series I bonds are the new kid on the block. They were first issued in 1998 and pay interest at a variable rate. If you do inherit an I bond and want to cash it in, be sure it's been owned for at least five years. I bond holders pay a penalty for cashing them in before then. If you cash them in before they are five years old, you forfeit the three most recent months' interest.

Question 69. How do you determine the value of property held as a co-ownership?

If the property to be transferred after your death is held with another person, it can greatly affect the value to be reported as part of your estate. The estate laws assume that one person is the sole owner of the property. If you have partial ownership, the value of that property may need to be adjusted based on that partial ownership. How that value is adjusted will be based on the type of co-ownership involved. Ownership can be by tenancy in common, joint tenancy with right of survival, and tenants by the entirety and community property. Each of these types of ownership is addressed separately in Questions 70 and 72.

Question 70. How do you determine the value of property held as tenancy in common?

When calculating the property value in this case, multiply the percentage ownership of the deceased in the property by the property's fair market value. As discussed in Questions 63 and 64, there may be some additional discounts if real estate or a business is involved.

Question 71. How do you determine the value of property held as joint tenancy with right of survival?

Valuation of this property depends upon whether the joint tenants are husband and wife. If the property is held by husband and wife, the ownership is considered to be one-half each, and one-half of the property value is included in the value of the estate. But if that joint tenancy was created before 1977, the spouse may use the rule for non-married joint tenants.

When determining the value of property in an estate involving non-married joint tenants with right of survivorship, the deceased tenant's share of that property is based on his or her proportional contribution to the original purchase price plus any improvement costs. The executor of the will must be able to prove the contribution of the surviving joint tenants or 100 percent of the value of the property must be included in the gross estate. If you do buy property with right of survival jointly with someone to whom you are not married, be sure to document how much you contributed to the purchase of that property, as well as any improvements made on that property, or you could end up having to pay estate taxes on money you contributed if you live the longest and inherit the property in its entirety.

Question 72. **How do you determine the value of property held as tenancy by the entirety and community property?**

Property held in this way can only be held by husband and wife. For this type of ownership, the co-owners are considered to own one-half the property, and the property value included in the estate of the deceased owner will be one-half the value of the property.

Question 73. **What date is used for the valuation of property?**

When an executor is determining the value of property in the estate, he has two possible dates from which to choose. The value of the property in the estate can be based on the value at the time of the death or it can be valued six months after the death.

In either case, the executor must value all property in the estate based on one of these two dates. For example, suppose the value of a stock portfolio dropped rapidly during the six months after a person's death. It may make sense to use the value date six months after the death to save taxes on the estate. But, if during that same time other assets, such a real estate, rose dramatically in price, then the executor would need to calculate the estate based on both dates to determine which date would result in the lowest tax liability. The executor must use the same date for valuing all the property. He can't choose one date for some of the property and the other date for the rest of the property.

Question 74. **How do you report and pay federal estate tax?**

Whether you have to file an estate tax return will depend on the value of the estate. If the value of the estate does not exceed the maximum applicable exclusion amount, which is $2 million in 2007 and 2008 and $3.5 million in 2009, then no tax return must be filed. In 2010, since the estate tax is fully repealed, no heirs who inherit an estate from someone who dies that year will have to file an estate tax return. But in 2011, unless the law is changed, you will need to file an estate tax return for any estate with a value over $1 million.

In many cases the executor or executrix is responsible for filing the tax returns. If all assets were transferred using will substitutes (see Chapter 5), the recipients of the assets will be responsible for filing the tax return.

An estate tax return is due nine months after the person's death, but often the full value of the estate is not known at that time. Sometimes the estate can include assets that take longer to determine the value, such as the assets of a small business owner. If more than nine months are needed, you can file for an automatic extension of six months by filling out IRS Form 4768. Any further extensions will require you to show cause for why you can't complete the forms.

Chapter 7

CALCULATING THE ESTATE TAX

Calculating estate taxes can be a mathematical nightmare. While the actual calculation of the tax can be done fairly simply using IRS tables, the reason estate tax computations are so difficult is due to the elements you must calculate to find the taxable amount. This chapter reviews the basics of what you must consider to calculate estate taxes.

Question 75. **What are the key parts of calculating estate tax?**

The actual calculation of the tax is simple once you find the value of the net estate. Getting to that value is where the complications arise. Here is the actual formula for finding your net estate tax due:

- Take the gross estate value, and subtract the amount allowed by deductions. This gives the taxable estate.
- Now add taxable lifetime transfers since 1976. This gives your tax base.

■ Next, multiply your tax base by the applicable estate tax rate. This gives your tentative estate tax.
■ Finally, subtract your credits to find your net estate tax due.

In the following questions I break down the key parts of this calculation and discuss how the estate tax calculation differs from the income tax calculation.

Question 76. What is the difference in calculating estate tax versus income tax?

The primary difference between income tax and estate tax calculations is how you determine your applicable tax rate. For income tax, you calculate your tax rate based on the level of income earned in a given year. For estate taxes, you need to calculate what remains in an estate as of the date of the decedent's death, and also add all cumulative taxable transfers of wealth throughout the decedent's lifetime since 1976 when the gift tax and estate tax were combined. That means any taxable gifts given to family over the years must be added as part of the total estate.

If the decedent's estate involves more than the current maximum allowed to be excluded from tax—$2 million in 2007 and 2008 and $3.5 million in 2009—you must be able to calculate how much was given in taxable gifts over the years as well as how much is left in the estate. Taxable gifts are gifts of more than $12,000 in any one year ($24,000 if a couple). The amount can be adjusted by the government annually for inflation. If taxes were already paid on these gifts, they can be subtracted as credits, so the estate is not taxed twice. You will face a big problem if proper records have not been kept and you can't perform this calculation.

Question 77. **What is the gross estate?**

The gross estate serves as the starting point for all estate tax calculations. While in many states, the gross estate is the same as the probate estate, this is not true at the federal level. In addition to the probate estate, you must add any items not included in probate, such as property transferred by will substitutes (see Chapter 5), insurance proceeds, and retirement benefits.

Question 78. **Which property is calculated in the gross estate?**

When trying to determine which property should be included in the gross estate, the key question to ask is whether the decedent was in possession of that property at death—no matter what kind of property is involved. The gross estate can include antiques, art, bank accounts, bonds, cars, certificates of deposit, contracts, house, leases, life insurance policies on the life of another, partnership interests, promissory notes, royalties, and stocks. All these assets must be included in the calculation of the gross estate. Even if the decedent only had a partial interest in any of these items, value for these items must be included in the gross estate. The valuation of property is covered in Chapter 6. For example, if the decedent owned community property with his wife, then one-half the value of that property must be included in the gross estate.

In addition, income that is not includable in the decedent's income tax returns for the year of his or her death must be calculated and included in the gross estate. This income is called income in respect of decedent (IRD) and includes bonuses, deferred compensation, expense reimbursements, interest accrued and payable to the decedent in the future, proceeds from installment sales, renewal commissions, and any other type of income that will be received by the estate in the future.

Question 79. **Is life insurance part of the gross estate?**

The insurance proceeds from any insurance policy owned by the decedent at death must be included in the gross estate. Even if the decedent does not own the life insurance policy outright (such as might be the case with policies owned by an employer), if the decedent had some incident of ownership, such as the right to name a beneficiary, then the proceeds must be included in the gross estate. Examples of incident of ownership include the right to borrow against the policy cash values; the right to cash in, surrender or cancel the policy; the right to pledge the policy as collateral for a loan; and the right to receive policy dividends.

You can avoid including insurance proceeds from a life insurance policy by assigning all incidents of ownership to an irrevocable life insurance trust. But you must set up this trust at least three years before your death in order for the proceeds to be left out of the estate.

Question 80. **How is joint property calculated in the gross estate?**

How joint property is calculated depends upon the type of joint ownership. Two types of ownership do not include the right of survivorship: tenancy in common and traditional community property. In these situations, the decedent is considered to have a fractional interest in the property, and that fractional interest is included in the gross estate.

If the ownership includes a right of survivorship, such as joint tenancy with right of survival or tenancy by the entirety, then the portion of the property included in the gross estate will be dependent on the relationship of the owners. If the joint owners are husband and wife, one-half of the value of the property is included in the gross estate no matter how much each spouse contributed to the property. There is an exception to this if the joint tenancy was created before 1977. In that case, the surviving spouse can choose to use the rules for joint owners who are not spouses.

For joint owners who are not spouses, the portion of the property's value that will be included in the decedent's estate will depend upon the decedent's contribution when the property was purchased. For example, if you can prove that the decedent only contributed 33 percent of the cost to purchase that joint property, then only 33 percent of the current value of the property would be included in the decedent's gross estate.

Question 81. **Are survivorship benefits (retirement benefits, pensions, annuities) included in the gross estate?**

Inclusion of survivorship benefits for retirement benefits, pensions, or annuities in the gross estate depends upon what happens to the value of those benefits upon the decedent's death. In some cases, the benefits for an annuity may end, and nothing will be added to the decedent's gross estate. If the benefits will be paid in a lump sum upon death, then the lump sum is added to the gross estate.

If the periodic benefits will continue to be paid after the decedent's death, then you must calculate the present value of those benefits. That present value should be added to the gross estate.

Formulas for calculating present value depend upon the type of annuity. If the annuity is a private annuity (any annuity issued by an entity other than an insurance company, such as an employer), use the interest set by the IRS, called the applicable federal rate, to calculate the present value. The IRS does publish valuation tables to make this calculation easier. For example, you can access the June 2007 rate table online at the IRS Web site *http://www.irs.gov/pub/irs-drop/rr-07-36.pdf*.

If the annuity is provided by a commercial insurance company, the present value is measured by the premium charged for a newly issued single life annuity on the survivor's life, which is the amount you would have to pay to buy the same type of annuity on the survivor's life.

Question 82. **Is property subject to a qualified conservation easement included in the gross estate?**

You can reduce the value of land to be added to your gross estate by up to 40 percent by setting up a qualified conservation easement. You give up the right to develop, improve, or modify the property in the easement.

To keep the value of this land out of your gross estate, you must:

- Own the land for a three-year period before your death.
- Make a qualified conservation contribution of the property in perpetuity to a qualified charitable organization.
- Maintain no development rights over the granted easement.

Preservation of a certified historic structure does not qualify as a conservation purpose for this estate tax exclusion. Also if there is still debt financing on this property, only the equity portion of the property value is eligible for the exclusion.

Question 83. **What are lifetime transfers, and how are they included in the gross estate?**

Even if you give away large portions of your estate prior to your death, those portions must still be included when calculating the gross estate. Each year you can give a gift of up to $12,000 to any person without having to worry about it being a taxable transfer for gift or estate tax purposes. A couple can give up to $24,000 to any individual. The annual exclusion amount can be adjusted by the government annually for inflation. Larger gifts are considered lifetime transfers and are taxable through gift taxes or estate taxes. Up to $1 million of taxable lifetime transfers are excluded from the gift tax, but any gifts above that level are taxed. When calculating the gross estate, all taxable lifetime transfers must be added to the calculation.

Question 84. **If a person retains a lifetime interest in property, is that included in the gross estate?**

If you transfer your property to a family member prior to your death but retain an interest in that property until your death, then the value of that property must be included in your gross estate. For example, suppose you give your home to your son or daughter but keep a life estate in the property (continue to control the property until your death). The value of the property will be calculated as part of your gross estate.

This is also true if you establish an irrevocable trust but keep the right to receive income from that trust while you are alive. You can stipulate that you will receive income from that trust for fifteen years, and as long as you die after the last payment, the value of the trust will not be included in your gross estate. But if you stipulate that the payments from the trust will continue until one month prior to your death, the trust value must be included in your gross estate. In fact, any measurement of your ownership in property that is based on your death will make that property subject to estate taxes.

Question 85. **What is retaining a reversionary interest and is it included in the gross estate?**

If you hold a reversionary interest in property that you give away, even if you haven't gotten that property back, the value of the property must be included in the gross estate. For example, suppose you gave another person a piece of property, and one of the provisions of that gift was that the property would revert to you if the recipient of the gift died before you. In this case, you still have sufficient control of the property for it to be considered property in which you have an interest, and it must be included in your gross estate.

Question 86. **What is retaining the rights to alter, terminate, revoke, or amend the transfer of property, and is
the property included in the gross estate?**

If you maintain any right to alter, terminate, revoke, or amend an
agreement that transfers property you own to another individual
or entity, that property must be included in the gross estate. For
example, if you set up a revocable trust and put property you own
in that trust, it is assumed you still have an interest in that property,
and the property's value must be included in your gross estate.

Question 87. **What is the three-year inclusionary rule?**

Even if you give property away, if that gift of property was within
three years of your death, it may still need to be included in your
gross estate. This is known as the three-year inclusionary rule, which
is sometimes known as the "transfers in contemplation of death"
rule. There are three basic parts to this rule:

1. *Transferring your retained interest in a property within three
    years of your death.* If you give up your rights to a life estate
    within three years of your death, the value of that property
    will still be included in your gross estate.
2. *Transfers of insurance.* If you transfer all incidents of ownership
    in a life insurance policy on your life to someone else within
    three years of your death, then the proceeds of the life insur-
    ance policy must be included in your gross estate.
3. *Gift taxes.* If you pay gift taxes on any gifts within three years
    of your death, these taxes are included in the gross estate.

Question 88. **What can be deducted from the gross
estate?**

Your gross estate can be reduced with many different kinds of
deductions. Common deductions include:

- Debts
- Funeral expenses
- Administrative expenses
- Casualty and theft losses
- State estate taxes paid
- Marital deduction
- Charitable deductions

After the first four deductions are subtracted, this is known as the adjusted gross estate. When the last three deductions are taken, this becomes the taxable estate. (More about what can be included in these deductions is discussed in Questions 89 to 96.)

Question 89. How are debts, mortgages, and liens deducted from the gross estate?

Any financial obligations owed by the decedent can be deducted from the gross estate. This includes accrued rent and lease payments, credit-card balances, open accounts at retailers, mortgages, promissory notes, and property liens, as well as any due but unpaid taxes.

Question 90. How do you calculate funeral expenses to be deducted from the gross estate?

As long as the funeral expenses are reasonable, they can be deducted from the estate. These reasonable expenses can include a headstone, even if it is somewhat extravagant; a burial plot and its future care; travel expenses of persons necessary for the ceremony; and the costs of a meal for guests after the ceremony.

Question 91. What administrative expenses can be deducted from the gross estate?

The cost of managing a decedent's estate can be high, and any reasonable expenses can be deducted from the gross estate. This can include the appraisal fees, attorneys' fees, insurance bills to protect the property until sold or distributed to heirs, personal representative's commission, probate fees, rent (e.g., to keep a retail establishment open until a business is sold or distributed to heirs), safekeeping fees (e.g., to pay security for the property or maintenance on the property if needed), trust fees, and utility bills.

The federal estate tax return is due nine months after the decedent's death. If the estate remains open and undistributed at that time, you can ask for a six-month extension or estimate what all the administrative expenses will be. You can also decide to claim any unclaimed administrative expenses on the final estate federal income tax return.

Question 92. **Can you deduct estate taxes paid to a foreign government?**

If you own property in another country, you may be subject to estate taxes by that foreign government. The U.S. government permits you to deduct these taxes provided that the property located in that foreign country is included in calculation for the gross estate in the United States or the property was transferred for public, charitable, or religious uses. While this deduction is available, few people use it. Instead they use a tax credit that is available in the credit section of the taxable estate calculation, which usually saves more money. (See Question 101 for more information.)

Question 93. **What theft and casualty losses can be deducted from the gross estate?**

You can deduct any theft or casualty losses incurred after the decedent's death, which are not covered by insurance, and before the distribution to beneficiaries or heirs. For example, if the decedent's house burns down before the estate is settled and the insurance on the home covers only 90 percent of the fair market value, the portion of the value not covered by the insurance company can be deducted from the gross estate.

Question 94. **What state estate taxes can be deducted from the gross estate?**

When the Economic Growth and Tax Relief Reconciliation Act of 2001 was passed in 2004, the credit for state estate taxes was killed, and a deduction was added instead. A deduction is worth less than a credit, because while a deduction reduces the amount of the gross estate, a credit reduces the amount of the taxes due. So you can deduct state estates taxes in 2007 to 2009. In 2010, it won't matter because if you die in 2010, there will be no federal estate taxes. But if you die after that time, and there is no change to the law, then the old estate tax law becomes law again, and the state estate tax credit can be used.

Question 95. **What is the marital deduction, and how is it calculated?**

If you give your entire estate, even if it's $100 million, to your surviving spouse, the marital deduction can erase the potential estate tax liability to zero, as long as the money transfers to your spouse in a qualified way. The best way to guarantee this deduction is to pass your property to your spouse through a will, beneficiary designation, or right of survivorship. This removes any chance of doubt that the property was passed in a qualified way.

If you die without a will and your spouse receives property under state intestacy law, doubts could arise. In most cases, your spouse would still be able to take the marital deduction—but why risk it? It's best to be sure all your property will transfer by drawing up a will, beneficiary designation, or survivorship.

The marital deduction can only be used by a marriage between one man and one woman. Marriages between same-sex couples are not recognized in federal law after the passage of the Defense of Marriage Act.

Question 96. **How much can be deducted in charitable contributions from the gross estate?**

The amount you can deduct for a charitable contribution is unlimited provided the charity qualifies under federal estate tax law. If the charity is a public charity, there is little doubt about qualification, because whether the charity qualifies for tax deductibility is publicly known. You may find it more difficult to prove qualification if the charity is a private foundation. The IRS publishes a list of charities that qualify for gift and estate tax purposes. If you want to make a charitable contribution in your will, contact the IRS before writing that will to be sure the charity qualifies for federal estate tax deductions.

The law allows this deduction for the contribution of cash or property only. You can't give a charity the right to use the property for free to get a deduction; you must actually give the charity title to the property.

Question 97. **What are adjusted taxable gifts, and how do they impact the calculation of the estate tax?**

All post-1976 gifts made by the decedent must be adjusted to remove the taxable portion of the gift. This is done by including gift items based on their value at the time of the gift, while other items in the gross estate are valued at fair market value at the decedent's death or six months after the death if that time frame is chosen. This can make a significant difference in the total of the gross estate, especially if the gift changed in value between the time it was given and the time of the decedent's death. For example, suppose parents gave their home to their child and moved to a smaller place. At the time of the gift, the home was worth $150,000, but at the time of the parents' death, the home was worth $300,000. Only the $150,000 would need to be included when calculating the gross estate and gift or estate taxes.

Any gift taxes paid on the gift are subtracted as a credit, so taxes won't be paid twice.

Question 98. **What is the gift taxes payable credit?**

Any gift taxes paid out of pocket for gifts given after 1976 can be subtracted from the gross estate tax. This gift taxes payable credit can only be taken if the decedent made taxable transfers of property during his or her lifetime that cumulatively exceeded the gift tax applicable exclusion amount in any one year. The exclusion amount in a year is $12,000 for an individual and $24,000 for a couple. The annual exclusion amount can be adjusted annually for inflation.

Question 99. **What is the applicable credit?**

The applicable credit is the full amount of an applicable credit allowed in the year of the decedent's death. You're entitled to the full credit because all gifts have been included in the gross amount of the estate. The following IRS charts show the 2007 federal tax rates for estates and trusts and the tax applicable exclusion amount.

2007 Federal Tax Rates for Estates and Trusts
Over $10,450

2007 Federal Estate and Trust Tax Rates

If taxable income is:	The tax is:
Not over $2,150	15% of the taxable income
Over $2,150 but not over $5,000	$322.50 plus 25% of the excess over $2,150
Over $5,000 but not over $7,650	$1,035 plus 28% of the excess over $5,000
Over $7,650 but not over $10,450	$1,777 plus 33% of the excess over $7,650
$2,701 plus 35% of the excess over $10,450	

Increased Estate Tax Applicable Exclusion Amount

An estate tax return for a U.S. citizen or resident needs to be filed only if the gross estate exceeds the applicable exclusion amount, listed here:

Applicable Exclusion Amounts

Year Exclusion	Amount
2006, 2007, and 2008	$2,000,000
2009	$3,500,000

Question 100. What is the credit for federal gift taxes?

This credit is allowed for any gift taxes paid out of pocket prior to 1977. The credit can also be taken for gift taxes paid out of pocket by the decedent's spouse on gifts for which the decedent was the donor but the gifts were split. The credit that can be taken is equal to the lesser of the gift tax or the estate tax paid on the property in question. The purpose of this credit is to avoid double taxation of transferred property.

Question 101. What is the credit for foreign estate taxes?

You can take this credit if you paid taxes on property to a foreign country that is located outside the United States, as long as the property is included in the gross estate in the United States. The credit is limited to the lesser of the foreign estate or the amount of the U.S. estate attributable to the property in question.

Question 102. **What is the prior transfer credit?**

To avoid double taxation, this credit is allowed on taxes paid for property received ten years before or two years after the death of the decedent. If the property was included in the taxable estate of the transferor and a beneficial interest in the property was transferred to the decedent, the decedent's estate does not need to include any interest in the property at death. This credit can be used even if the decedent sold the property or gave it to charity.

Chapter **8**

ESTATE TAX PLANNING

Chapter 7 presented the key factors that go into calculating gift and estate taxes. This chapter focuses on minimizing the estate taxes that will need to be paid on your estate. Through various types of trusts, you can significantly reduce your estate taxes.

Question 103. What are the goals of estate tax planning?

There are three important reasons to do estate tax planning:

1. To lower the value of your gross estate
2. To increase the deductions your estate will be eligible for or entitled to take
3 To maintain the estate's eligibility for as many credits as possible

These may sound obvious, but they're not always easy to attain. Consult an estate tax planner to be sure the strategies you plan to use will actually work when the taxes are calculated on your estate.

Question 104. **How can you reduce the gross estate?**

You can reduce your gross estate by giving away assets during your lifetime. However, to avoid ending up with the full value of these assets included in your estate, you must give them away more than three years before your death. The three-year inclusionary rule (see Question 87) could force those assets to be included in your gross estate. You also must give the property away without retaining any rights for the strategy to work.

While it is true that you must include the value of gifts in your gross estate, a gift of property more than three years before your death is included based on the value of that gift at the time it was given rather than at the time of your death. For example, suppose you gave your son or daughter the title to property worth $100,000 in 2000. At the time of your death, that property has jumped in value to $300,000. When calculating the estate, the property value would be $100,000 not $300,000. Had you held on to that property, the gross estate would have to include the higher $300,000 value.

Question 105. **How can you preserve or increase the estate tax deductions and credits?**

There are three tools that can help you preserve or increase your estate tax deduction and credits. They are as follows:

1. *Marital deduction.* This deduction is unlimited for any property you leave to your spouse. Any assets given to the spouse can delay taxation until after the death of the surviving spouse.
2. *Charitable deduction.* The deduction is unlimited for any property you leave to a qualified charity. The IRS publishes a list of qualified charities for federal estate tax purposes. Be sure the charity you pick is on that list.
3. *Applicable credit amount.* You can end up giving too much of your estate to your spouse or a charity without taking full advantage of the applicable credit amount.

Basically in planning your estate, be sure to consider the applicable credit amount before increasing your deductions with marital or charitable deductions. Otherwise you can end up writing off all taxes when the first spouse dies and paying even more taxes on the total estate when the surviving spouse dies because the marginal tax rate is higher.

Question 106. How do you manage the marital deduction for estate tax planning purposes?

There are no taxes on gifts between spouses. The IRS allows transfers between husband and wife without any taxable event for gift or estate tax purposes because the IRS sees the couple as one economic entity rather than two. The use of a marital deduction does not eliminate the payment of estate taxes, it just delays it.

Trusts generally cannot be used to minimize future taxes that must be paid on the marital estate when the second spouse dies, even though the marital deduction can delay those taxes. When managing the assets used as part of a marital deduction, trusts are often used for non-tax reasons, including:

- Some trusts give the spouse who grants the trust control over who will get the assets after the spouse who receives the trust dies. For example, suppose the husband wants to give his second wife a trust that she can use while she is alive but wants to give children from his first marriage rights to the remaining funds in the trust. He could accomplish this through a qualified terminable property trust (QTIP). (I talk more about the QTIP trust in Question 109 and the bypass trust, another way of handling such situations, in Question 110.)
- If set up properly, a trust can protect assets from the claims of the beneficiaries' creditors.
- Trusts provide for professional management of assets, which might offer more expertise than the individual beneficiary may have.

Question 107. **What is the power of appointment trust (marital trust)?**

This is a common type of marital trust where the recipient spouse gets an income interest for life and the power to decide where the remaining funds should go either during her lifetime or after her death. If the trust is given as a gift during her lifetime, then gift taxes apply. Any money left in the trust at the recipient spouse's death would be subject to estate tax.

This type of marital trust is used if the spouse establishing the trust:

- Desires to leave the funds in trust rather than as an outright transfer of assets. (In this case, a professional would manage the assets of the trust.)
- Decides to use the marital deduction for these assets
- Wants to give his or her spouse the maximum possible control over the assets
- Does not care if the recipient spouse changes the person who will receive any remaining funds after the death of the recipient spouse

Question 108. **What is an estate trust?**

In this trust, the spouse who establishes the trust names her surviving spouse as the sole beneficiary of the trust. Any income or money left in the trust at the end of the recipient spouse's lifetime would be distributed based on the provisions of the recipient spouse's will. The primary difference between this type of trust and a power of appointment trust is that income paid to the recipient spouse is discretionary and not mandatory. The trustee makes a determination about when to pay the recipient spouse income and how much that income should be.

The biggest advantage is that this trust qualifies for the marital deduction but doesn't make it mandatory to pay the recipient spouse anything. Although rarely used, if a couple wants to get full advantage of the marital deduction yet leave all the money in the trust for their children, this is one possible vehicle to make that happen. The recipient spouse maintains full control over whom to leave the money to through his will.

Question 109. **What is the QTIP trust?**

The qualified terminable property trust (QTIP) is similar to the power of appointment trust in how income is paid to the recipient spouse, but its key difference is that the spouse establishing the trust decides who will get any trust funds remaining after the death of the recipient spouse. So the spouse establishing the trust maintains more control of the money then he would with a power of appointment trust. This trust qualifies for the marital deduction but leaves the distribution of assets to the discretion of the personal representative, who can decide to use the marital deduction for part or all of the trust assets. Use this trust if you want:

- To leave property in trust rather than as an outright transfer
- To enable flexibility about whether the marital deduction should be used for the trust funds
- To ensure that your spouse will receive mandatory income for the rest of his or her life
- To be sure that you can name the recipient of any remaining funds in the trust after the death of your spouse

Question 110. **What is bypass planning?**

To be certain that the appropriate amount of the estate does not fall under a marital or charitable deduction, which would use up a portion of the estate tax exclusion, a bypass trust can be used. This type of trust will not qualify for the marital deduction, because it will name the surviving spouse as just one of several income beneficiaries of the trust. As indicated earlier, it's important not to waste the estate tax applicable exclusion, because then all the assets that go to the surviving spouse become taxable. By adding both the husband's and wife's shares and putting all the assets in one pot at the death of the first spouse, the tax margin could be a lot higher when the surviving spouse dies.

Use a bypass trust if you

- Want to leave property in trust rather than as an outright transfer
- Do not want to use the marital deduction for the assets placed in the trust
- Want to include more than just your spouse as income beneficiaries
- Want to control who will get the assets at the death of your spouse

Question 111. **What strategies can be used to combine marital and bypass trusts?**

If you know that you will have to pay estate taxes, one of the best ways to minimize or delay those taxes is a combination of both marital and bypass trusts. Use the bypass trust to use up your estate tax applicable exclusion and then put the remaining assets in a marital trust, such as the power of appointment trust, to protect the rest of your assets from immediate estate taxes. Since this trust qualifies for the marital deduction, all assets in that trust will not be taxed until the death of the surviving spouse.

If you want your surviving spouse to have less control of the assets and not argue about who should get those assets after his or her death, then use the QTIP trust rather than the power of appointment trust. Often a combination of the three trusts will be used, which will allow the surviving spouse full control of the power of appointment trust but leave the disbursement of the assets in the QTIP trust to the trustee to ensure money will be there for the children and grandchildren.

Question 112. **How do you use the charitable deduction in estate tax planning?**

The simplest way is to transfer the assets completely through a fee simple title to the cash or property you want to leave to the charity. But, often a person wants to leave only a partial interest in those assets. To make a partial charitable contribution that will meet the requirements of the charitable deduction, there are several types of trusts you can use including the remainder trust, the charitable lead trust, and the charitable remainder annuity trust. (See Questions 113 to 116 for a review of these types of trusts.) All these types of trusts guarantee that the charity will get some part of the property in the trust for which the deduction is allowed.

Question 113. **What is the remainder trust in a farm or personal residence?**

Use a remainder trust if you want to make provisions for your farm or personal residence to be donated to a charity but guarantee that your surviving spouse can live on the farm or in the residence for the remainder of her or his life. The value of this property would then qualify for the charitable deduction.

If the person named to have the life estate is your spouse, the marital deduction would initially be used to avoid estate taxes upon your death. Upon the death of the surviving spouse, the charitable deduction would then be used. The allowable charitable deduction would be computed using the appropriate IRS tables and applicable federal rate.

Question 114. **What is a charitable lead trust?**

If you want to leave an income for one of your favorite charities for a set number of years and then name a recipient for the remaining trust assets, you can use a charitable lead trust. The charity has first priority over the income interest in the trust. The trust is irrevocable and can last for a specified number of years, for your life, or for the life of a specified person who must be living at the time the trust is established.

To qualify for the charitable deduction, you must set up guaranteed annuity from the trust assets or a fixed percentage of the value of the assets. If the trust's interest income does not meet the guaranteed amount, the rest of the payment must be taken from the trust's principal. The charitable deduction is then calculated by finding the present value of the income stream using the IRS actuarial tables and the applicable federal rate.

Question 115. What is a charitable remainder trust?

You may decide to make provisions for a portion of your remaining assets to go to charity, but you want some other beneficiary, who is not a charity, to receive some portion of the assets first. You can do this by establishing a charitable remainder trust. Initially the interest income would go to the non-charitable beneficiaries, and any remaining assets would go to the charity. This type of trust is irrevocable and can last for the lifetime of the named non-charity beneficiaries or for a specified number of years, which cannot exceed twenty.

Congress added requirements in 1997 to establish charitable remainder trusts that qualify for the charitable deduction. For the trust to qualify, the annuity payment in any one year cannot be more than 50 percent of the initial fair market value of the trust, or the percentage specified cannot be more than 50 percent of the trust. Also the value of any remainder interest must be at least 10 percent of the fair market value of the trust assets on the date the trust is established. These new provisions were added to ensure some of the trust's assets actually go to the charity.

Question 116. **What are a charitable remainder annuity trust and a charitable remainder unitrust?**

The primary difference is the way in which the ongoing payments to the beneficiaries of the trust are calculated. With a charitable remainder annuity trust (CRAT), the payment to beneficiaries is a set sum that cannot be less than 5 percent of the initial fair market value of the trust assets. With a charitable remainder unitrust (CRUT), the payments to beneficiaries are a fixed percentage that must be at least 5 percent. Any time the interest income of the trust does not meet the payout requirements, the principal of the trust must be used. A fixed percentage, such as that used in the CRUT, can be more risky if you want to be certain that the principal assets are not used.

Question 117. **What are pooled income funds?**

Pooled income funds, which must be established by a public charity, are a type of charitable remainder trust that pools your donated assets with others' assets. These funds are used by people who want to take advantage of the estate tax charitable deduction using a charitable remainder trust but don't have enough assets to warrant the costs of setting up an individual trust.

When a decedent's estate transfers property to the fund, the decedent's will can specify that one or more individuals who are alive at the time of the transfer will get a life income interest in the property transferred. The remaining value of the property then becomes a charitable contribution; the charity involved has an irrevocable vested remainder interest in the property. The income interest paid to the named beneficiaries is paid out as a percentage of the total contributed by their donor/decedent. When the income beneficiaries die, the principal amount remaining is passed to the public charity.

Question 118. **What is a qualified funeral trust?**

Funeral expenses can be deducted from your gross estate. One way to set aside these expenses while you are still alive and be sure that they will be deductible is to establish a qualified funeral trust. For this trust to meet the requirements, it must:

- Result from a contract with a person in the trade or business of providing funeral or burial services
- Have the sole purpose to hold, invest, and reinvest funds in the trust and to use these funds for the sole purpose of paying for funeral or burial services for the benefit of the beneficiaries of the trust
- Permit only beneficiaries who are named in the trust to be provided services upon their death under the specified contract with the funeral company
- Be set up specifically for the purpose of a qualified funeral trust. (You can't designate a trust set up for another purpose as a qualified funeral trust after the person's death to avoid taxes.)
- Be owned by the purchasers of the contract

Chapter 9

RULES ON GIVING— FEDERAL GIFT TAX

You may want to give away your assets while you are alive so you can watch your beneficiaries and heirs enjoy them. Be careful, because sizable gifts are not completely tax free. Chapter 8 focused on gift and estate taxes. In this chapter, I review what a gift is and the nuances of how you can give a gift to minimize those taxes.

Question 119. What is a gift?

A gift can include money or property, including the use of property, that is given without expecting to receive something of equal value in return. You may also be making a gift if you sell something at less than its value or make an interest-free or reduced-interest loan. The IRS takes a very broad view of whether an asset is a gift. The federal gift tax applies to any completed direct or indirect lifetime transfer of property by a competent donor for less than the full or adequate consideration in money. That means, the IRS can determine something is a gift even if you did not intend it to be. The person receiving the gift doesn't have to pay taxes on it but will have to pay taxes on any income generated by the gift. The person giving the gift may have to pay gift or estate taxes on it.

Certain intrafamily transactions can actually end up being gifts when you didn't intend them to be. Here are some common situations to watch out for to avoid giving a gift when you don't intend to do so:

- *Forgiveness of a legally enforceable debt.* Parents often given their children a loan to go to school, buy a house, or start a business. If you forgive the loan, and this loan exceeds the maximum allowable amount in a given year, you could end up owing gift taxes.
- *Intrafamily loans.* Parents or family members often make a loan to another family member at an interest rate considerably below what would be charged at a bank. If the amount of interest saved would be more than the allowable amount in a given year, you could end up owing gift taxes.
- *Bargain sales.* Sometimes an older family decides to sell an asset to a younger family member at a price well below market value. This can be considered a bargain sale, and you may have to pay a gift tax on the difference between what the younger family member pays and the market value of the asset.

You can give up to $12,000 in 2007—$24,000 as a couple—without having to worry about paying taxes on the gift. This amount is adjusted annually for inflation. Cumulatively over your lifetime, you can give up to $1 million without having to pay gift taxes, but the amount of the gifts you give will be added to the value of your gross estate.

There are some exceptions to the tax rules on gifts. The following types of gifts do not count against your annual gift-giving limit:

- Tuition or medical expenses that you pay directly to an education institution or medical institution for someone's benefit
- Gifts to your spouse
- Gifts to a political organization for its use
- Gifts to charities

If you receive a gift in exchange for services, it is not considered a gift and should be reported as income. You do not have to report the receipt of a true gift on your income taxes.

Question 120. How do you calculate the fair market value of gifts?

Generally the fair market value of a gift is calculated based on the value of the gift on the date of transfer. If you undervalue the gift on your gift tax return by 50 percent or more, you can be penalized for that undervaluation. The IRS states that the fair market value of a gift is "the price at which property would change hands between a willing buyer and a willing seller, neither being under a compulsion to buy or sell and both having reasonable knowledge of the relevant facts. The fair market value of a particular item of property includible in the decedent's gross estate is not to be determined by a forced sale price. Nor is the fair market value of an item of property to be determined by the sale price of the item in a market other than that in which such item is most commonly sold to the public, taking into account the location of the item wherever appropriate." In other words, for most gifts the fair market value equals the retail price at which the gift could have been purchased on the open market. (Chapter 6 discusses the calculation of fair market value for various types of assets.)

Question 121. **What are the filing requirements for gifts?**

When you make a gift that is subject to the gift tax, you must file IRS Form 709. If a couple makes a gift, each person must file this form. There is no such thing as filing a gift tax return jointly. If you do make a gift jointly and it is less than two times the maximum annual exclusion amount ($24,000 in 2007), your spouse may signify consent to split the gift without filing a separate form.

In addition to filing Form 709, you must attach these documents, if appropriate:

- Copies of transfer documents, such as deeds or trusts
- Statements from the insurance companies on Form 712, Life Insurance Statement, for each insurance policy listed on Form 709
- Financial documentation if the gift transfer involves a closely held business interest
- Professional appraisals of assets, especially if real estate is involved in the transfer

You file your gift tax return on the same date as your income tax return. For example, if you make a large gift in June, it does not have to be reported until April 15 of the next year. The only time this deadline may be different is if the gift tax return is being filed after a death. In that case, the federal estate tax return must be filed within nine months after the death unless a six-month extension is requested. The gift tax return must be filed at the same time as the estate tax return, if it is due before April 15.

Question 122. **What are special valuations for intrafamily transfers?**

Valuation on gifts involving intrafamily transfers can be particularly difficult to prove satisfactorily to the government when they involve a closely held business. In fact, four sections of the gift and estate tax codes are concerned with how to value intrafamily transfers.

Section 2701 applies specifically to transfers relating to corporate or partnership interests when there is no established market for such interests. Section 2702 applies to transfers in trust or transfers of term interests. Term interests include any interest that will last only for a specified amount of time or a lifetime. (Trusts and term interests are discussed further in Question 124.) Section 2703 applies to restrictions on the right to acquire, use, or sell property at less than fair market value or in a buy-sell agreement among business partners. (Buy-sell agreements are presented in Question 125.) Section 2704 applies to liquidation issues. If you are planning to make a gift to a family member, work with a financial adviser or attorney familiar with the intrafamily transfer laws. The government pays close attention to these types of transfers because of the valuation games some taxpayers have played. Penalties can be high if you don't value these gifts appropriately.

Question 123. **How is the valuation for purposes of gift taxes determined on lifetime transfers?**

When valuing a lifetime transfer for the purposes of gift taxes, three basic situations must exist for this type of intrafamily transfer to be legitimate:

1. There must be a gratuitous transfer, which is a transfer of property other than at fair market value.
2. The donor and the donee must be related.
3. The donor or a member of the donor's family must retain ownership interest in what is given away.

You cannot use the rules of Section 2701 and 2702 if the transfer involves a sale, a transaction between strangers, or the transfer of the donor's (and all applicable family members') entire interest in the asset.

In valuing this type of transfer for the purposes of gift taxes when the donor gives only part of his or her interest in the asset, subtract the value of what the donor has retained from what he or she owned prior to the transfer. This method of determining value is called the subtraction method. Under certain conditions, the IRS can rule that the value of the property retained is zero, and you must pay gift taxes on the entire value of what was owner prior to the transaction. So don't try to do this type of transfer on your own. Seek professional advice.

Question 124. **How is the valuation calculated on retained interests trusts and term interests?**

When transferring interests in trust or by a term interest, the gift tax value is determined by the subtraction method, as discussed in Question 123. This does apply if the property transferred into the trust is a personal residence used by the beneficiaries of the trust. Whether the retained interests will be valued at zero or at the value found by using the subtraction method will depend upon whether the interest meets the definition of a qualified interest. If the transferor and applicable family members hold control of the entity (50 percent of the stock or partnership interest) and the transferor and applicable family members retain liquidation, put, call, or conversion rights, then the retained interests are nonqualified and will be valued at zero.

For the IRS to consider that the donor or applicable family member has a retained interest of more than zero, which would mean they have a qualified interest, the retained right must give the donor something of economic value that will be subject to estate or gift tax at some future point. The IRS wants to ensure that the entire value of the asset will be subject to transfer tax at least once.

Question 125. **What is the effect of buy-sell agreements, options, and restrictions on valuation on the gift tax?**

Buy-sell agreements can help to transfer property at less than fair market value, provided that they can be proven to be a bona fide business arrangement. While this can be more easily done when strangers are involved, they can also be used with intrafamily transfers. The key things you must prove for a buy-sell agreement, option, or any other restriction on the right to acquire property at less than fair market value when intrafamily transfers are involved include:

- The arrangement cannot be simply an attempt to transfer property to a family member for less than the full and adequate consideration in money.
- The terms of the agreement you draft with the family member must be similar to arrangements that would be made by persons in an arm's-length transaction. An arm's-length transaction is defined as a transaction between two parties that is conducted as though they were not related and there is no question of a conflict of interest.

Question 126. **How are lapsing rights or restrictions treated under gift tax rules?**

Sometimes in a complicated intrafamily transfer of a closely held business, there will be a lapse of rights or restrictions. When this happens, the period of the lapse can be considered a gift.

For example, suppose a person gets 5 percent of the income of a family business, and there is a lapse of rights for two months. The income received during those two months would be considered part of the lapse and could be subject to gift taxes if the income exceeds the allowable gift tax exclusion of $12,000.

If a transfer includes a lapse in voting or liquidation rights and the individual who holds the right, along with members of the family, controls the entity both before and after the lapse, then the lapse is treated as a gift or a transfer includable in the gross estate of the individual holding the right. When determining the value of a transferred interest in a closely held business, restrictions on liquidation are ignored unless they are required by federal or state law or a commercially reasonable restriction that arises as part of financing the business.

Question 127. **What is a lifetime transfer, and when is it complete?**

A lifetime transfer is a transfer of a portion of ownership during a person's lifetime to the intended heir, but with the retention of some benefits from that asset. A lifetime transfer can be a valuable tool for closely held family businesses. Suppose the owner transfers the business to her children or other family members but retains a source of income for herself and continues to consult with the successors regarding the operation of the business. This can create a problem for estate tax purposes, so it's important that it is clearly stated when the donor relinquishes all dominion and control over the gifted property (a business, trust, or other asset). As long as the donor reserves certain powers over the gift, it is not considered complete. For a lifetime transfer to be considered complete, the donor must give up the power to change beneficiaries or alter the proportionate shares of beneficiaries.

When trying to determine the value of a gift, two things must be considered: the date the gift was completed and the nature of the gifted asset. This can become very convoluted when a lifetime transfer is involved.

In some situations, an ownership interest can be held in a completed gift. For example, if a father makes a gift of his business to his son but retains a life estate interest in the gift in the form of continuing income, it can be considered a completed gift for gift tax purposes as long as the father transfers title and all control to the son.

The timing of a gift's completion can be critical because the value of the gift will be based on the date of transfer. If you expect an asset to continue to increase in value, you want to lock in the earliest possible date for transfer. If you don't complete the gift prior to your death, the transfer date for the purposes of valuing the transfer will be the date of death or six months after the death, depending upon the date chosen by your personal representative.

Question 128. **How does adding your child's name to property impact the gift tax?**

A common practice to avoid probate is to add your child's name to the title of property, such as the parental home. If you do add your child's name as a joint tenant with right of survivorship, then you've given your child a gift, and that gift may be subject to gift taxes if its value exceeds the maximum amount of the annual exclusion.

Another common practice is for an elderly person to add the name of a child or other relative to a joint bank account so the younger person can help pay the bills. This means that either person has a right to the money in the account. As long as the child or other younger person put on the account only writes out checks to pay the bills of the older person, then the money will not be considered a gift. But if the younger person uses the money for himself or herself, that amount could be subject to gift tax if it exceeds the allowable annual exclusion.

Question 129. **What is a defective disclaimer?**

Sometimes you may get a gift and decide you don't want it either because you don't want the value of the gift to be included in your estate at death or you want someone else to get the gift. Whatever the reason, if you get a gift you don't want, you must prepare a qualified disclaimer to refuse the gift. If you reject the gift without meeting the requirements of the IRS, you will have to pay gift or estate taxes on it anyway when you give it to someone else. To avoid writing a defective disclaimer, here are the key parts of a qualified disclaimer:

- You must refuse the gift in writing.
- You must refuse the gift within nine months by sending the refusal to the donor or the legal representative of the donor.
- You must not accept the interest in the asset or any of its benefits.

- You may not have any say in who gets the asset instead of you.
- Your refusal must be irrevocable and unqualified.

Question 130. **What transfers of property are exempt from the gift tax?**

There aren't many transfers of property that are exempt from the gift tax, but a few do exist. These include:

- Transfers to political organizations
- Payments that qualify for an educational exemption (see Question 131)
- Payments that qualify for a medical exemption (see Question 132)

Medical and educational payments that qualify for the exemptions are unlimited in amount and do not have to be counted against the allowable maximum exclusion for gift tax purposes. These types of payments can be made even if you are not related to the person receiving the payments.

Question 131. **What qualifies as an educational exemption?**

The payment must be paid on behalf of an individual to a qualifying domestic or foreign organization. Education organizations that qualify must maintain a regular facility and curriculum and have a regularly enrolled student body in attendance where the educational activities take place. The payment must also be made directly to the institution and not to the individual for the purpose of tuition. You can't use this exemption for buying books or supplies. Nor can you use it for dormitory fees, board, or other similar expenses related to getting an education if these expenses are not specifically direct tuition payments. Any money given, even if given directly to the institution, for other educational costs will be considered a gift and could be subject to the gift tax if the amount exceeds the allowable annual maximum exclusion.

Question 132. **What qualifies as a medical exemption?**

The payment must be made on behalf of an individual directly to a medical care provider or institution that provided medical care for the individual. Medical care expenses can include diagnosis, cure, mitigation, treatment, or prevention of disease. The payments can also cover the cost of transportation primarily for and essential to the medical care. You can also pay the costs of medical insurance for an individual and qualify for the medical exemption, provided you make the payments directly to the insurance company. You cannot pay for medical care that would normally be paid by the individual's medical insurance. If you do make payments toward services that would normally be covered by insurance, those payments would be considered a gift and could be subject to the gift tax if the amount exceeds the allowable annual maximum exclusion.

Question 133. **How do you calculate total calendar-year gifts?**

When filing your taxes for any given year in which you have given gifts to others, make a list of those gifts. If the total gift to any one person exceeds the allowable annual maximum exclusion of $12,000 in 2007, you will be liable for gift taxes. Since you are allowed to give away a total of $1 million in gifts over your lifetime without paying taxes, you will have to report the gift but won't actually have to pay any taxes unless you've exceeded your $1 million limit. In addition to the allowable annual maximum exclusion, you can also reduce your gift tax obligation by splitting the gift with your spouse (see Question 134).

Question 134. **How can you split gifts with your spouse?**

You can split in half with your spouse the value of any gift you give to a third party so long as you haven't already given your spouse a general power of appointment over the gifted property. With gift splitting, a couple can give up to $24,000 in 2007 without having to worry about gift taxes. To qualify for gift splitting:

- Each spouse must be a U.S. citizen at the time of the gift.
- You must be married to each other at the time of the completion of the gift. If you do divorce, you cannot remarry during the remainder of the calendar year to avoid gift taxes.
- Each spouse must give his or her consent to the gift. You can do this by signifying consent on the other spouse's gift tax return or on your own gift tax return.

Question 135. **What is the annual exclusion?**

The annual exclusion is an amount that you can deduct from your gifts that will not be subject to the gift tax. You get this exclusion each year, and it is not cumulative from year to year.

In 2007 that exclusion is a maximum of $12,000, and it is adjusted each year, if the government deems it necessary, for inflation. The adjustment must be in multiples of $1,000, so it make take several years between adjustments before the government will decide it's necessary to make one. The exclusion is set by the next lowest multiple. The last time the exclusion amount was adjusted— from $11,000, which was set in 2002, to $12,000 in 2005—it took three years for the change to happen.

For a gift to qualify for this annual exclusion there must be a present value to the donee. You can't use the exclusion if the gift does not grant the donee present use of the money or other asset. For example, cash, a gift of a life estate in property, or a gift that involves a fee-simple interest in property could be considered gifts with present value. A gift of a remainder interest in property at some point would not qualify for the annual exclusion.

Question 136. **What are gift tax deductions?**

After you've take an exclusion for each of the gifts you are allowed, you may still be able to use one of two gift tax deductions to minimize your gift tax liability: the marital deduction (to find out what qualifies, see Question 137) and the charitable (to find out what qualifies, see Question 138). As with the federal estate tax, both of the deductions are unlimited and can erase your gift tax liability.

Question 137. **What qualifies for the marital deduction of gift taxes?**

Your spouse can receive gifts from you in an unlimited amount. The only limits on a marital gift involve the type of interest given. To fully qualify for the marital deduction, there are some limitations to how the gift is given.

- You must be married at the time of the gift. For federal tax purposes, since the Defense of Marriage Act was passed in 1996, a qualified marriage is one between a man and a woman. A same-sex married couple does not qualify.
- The spouse you make the gift to must be a U.S. citizen.
- The gift must be included in the donor's total calendar-year gifts.
- The donee spouse cannot be given a terminable interest for the gift for it to qualify.

A terminable interest is one that will end after a period of time or is based on some contingency. But, as long as an interest in the property in question is not given to someone else, the IRS usually will allow the marital deduction.

- The donee is given a qualified interest in the property for life.

Question 138. **What qualifies for the charitable deduction of gift taxes?**

You can give millions of dollars to charity, and all of it will be free of any federal gift tax. There are no limits to the amount of money or other assets you can donate to charity as long as the charity is on the IRS list of acceptable charities. Private operating foundations and charitable trusts will be more carefully scrutinized by the IRS, but they can still qualify. To qualify for the charitable deduction, there are some limitations on how the money can be given.

- You can only use the charitable deduction on cash or property. You can't use it on time or talent.
- The total of your gift can only be based on any value above what you may have received from a charity in return.
- Transfer cannot be one of partial interest, but the gift and estate code provides for some exceptions. (See Question 155 for more information on a partial interest charitable donation.)
- You can only claim the deduction for the calendar year in which you completed the gift.
- The property for which the deduction is taken must be included in the donor's total calendar-year gifts.

Chapter **10**

GENERATION-SKIPPING TRANSFER TAX

You may think you can avoid paying gift or estate taxes by passing property to a grandchild, but you can't. In 1976 Congress found that families were skipping a generation by naming grandchildren on trusts and other assets. So, to be sure that some transfer tax, either gift or estate tax, was collected in every generation, the generation-skipping transfer tax (GSTT) was born. Congress's first attempt to pass a law in 1976 didn't work. A second attempt at designing a GSTT in 1985 became law and is still on the books today. This chapter explains the tax and how it might affect your family.

Question 139. **What is the generation-skipping transfer tax?**

A generation-skipping tax covers the situation when wealth is not transferred from one generation to the next but instead is transferred two or more generations in the future. For example, suppose you decide to give a sizable gift of $200,000 to your grandchild. You would have to pay both the gift taxes and the GSTT on that gift.

You can avoid paying any gift taxes by applying that gift to your applicable credit amount of $1 million over your lifetime in gift taxes. You can still skip generations by giving money to your great- or great-great-grandchildren, or any person who is more than one generation younger than you, because a gift tax is only applied once even if you skip more than one generation with your gift. You won't be subject to GSTT if you pay medical or educational expenses directly for any person who is more than one generation younger than you.

Question 140. What is the difference between a skip person and a non-skip person?

You may find when discussing estate strategies with your financial adviser that she uses the term skip person or non-skip person. A skip person is two or more generations younger than you or your spouse. Anyone who does not fit the definition of a skip person is considered a non-skip person.

While you might think that generation assumes a blood rela- tionship, it doesn't for the purposes of the generation-skipping transfer tax. The only thing the law considers is how many genera- tions there are between the person giving the gift and the person receiving it. If generations are determined by age and not blood relationships, then for the GSTT to apply, any person receiving funds must be more than 37½ years younger (the period that the law defines as a "generation") than the transferor.

A spouse or former spouse is always considered to be in the same generation, and GSTT does not become a factor when assets are transferred. Also charitable entities are not a factor when con- sidering the GSTT.

Another exception that rules out the need for GSTT involves a family situation where a parent or grandparent dies. A child can move closer in generation to the living, and GSTT would not be a factor in the gift. For example, suppose a grandparent made a transfer to a grandchild, because his or her child had already died. The grandchild would not be considered a skip-person because after the death of his parent he moved one generation closer to the grandparent.

Two other key terms than impact GSTT are direct skips and indirect skips. The issues involving these terms are covered in Questions 141 and 142.

Question 141. **What is a direct skip?**

A direct skip is any transfer to a person who is a skip person, and it will be subject to gift tax or federal estate tax. If the property is transferred to a trust, the trust will only be considered a direct skip if the only people named in the trust are skip persons. In these situations, the assets in the trust would be subject to gift or federal estate taxes. You can't avoid the GSTT by naming a non-skip person in the trust solely for the purpose of trying to avoid GSTT. For example, if a grandparent names a parent as custodian for a minor child, the naming of the parent would not satisfy the requirement of a non-skip person, and the gift would still be subject to gift or federal estate taxes as well as GSTT.

You must report a gift made by direct skip on a gift tax return in the year that the transfer is completed, if the gift is made while transferor is still alive, which means by April 15 of the next year. If the transferor is deceased, then the gift will be reported on the federal estate tax return.

Question 142. **What is an indirect skip?**

An indirect skip involves a transfer of assets where at least one skip person and one non-skip person have an interest in the property after the transfer is complete. For example, suppose you are a grandparent and leave a life interest in your estate to your children and a remainder interest to your grandchild. That would be an indirect skip. Your children are non-skip persons, and your grandchild, who is removed from you by two generations, is a skip person. To qualify as an indirect skip, the non-skip person must have a current right to receive income or assets from the transfer.

Any GSTT that may be due on an indirect skip does not usually coincide with the federal gift or estate tax that may otherwise be due on a direct skip. The GSTT on indirect skips cannot be determined when a transfer is completed because it is not known at the time of transfer how much of the assets will go to the non-skip person or persons and how much will go to the skip person or persons. Only the portion of the transfer that goes to the skip person or persons is subject to the GSTT. Therefore the GSTT can only be calculated when the non-skip person's interest is either terminated or a taxable distribution of the property is made.

Question 143. **What is the GSTT exemption?**

Unless you are very wealthy, you won't have to worry about the GSTT, thanks to the lifetime exemption from this tax. This exemption allows you to make taxable generation-skipping transfers during your lifetime and at death in the amount equal to the estate tax applicable exclusion, which is $2 million in 2007 and 2008 and $3.5 million in 2009. In 2010, there is no estate tax, so there won't be any GSTT, but if the Congress doesn't act, the old law will go back into effect. If this happens, the GSTT will be restored to a base amount of $1 million that will be indexed to inflation by the next lowest multiple of $10,000.

Question 144. **How do you calculate the GSTT?**

The GSTT is calculated by determining the taxable amount, which is the value of the property received by the transferee times the applicable estate tax rate at the time of the transfer if a direct skip. If it's an indirect skip, multiply the value of the property received by the transferee by the applicable estate tax at the time the value to the skip persons can be determined. The taxable amount can be reduced by any deduction that is authorized in Section 2053 of the estate tax, which includes reasonable funeral and administration expenses, certain state and federal estate taxes, debts of the decedent, and liens against property included in the gross estate. But to take these deductions, the value of the property received must be reduced by the deductions. Any tax advice and tax return preparation fees you pay can also be deducted from the amount received as part of the tax calculation.

Question 145. What is the applicable rate for the GSTT?

The applicable rate for generation-skipping taxes is the same as the federal estate tax rate, which is 45 percent from 2007 to 2009. There will be no tax in 2010. If Congress doesn't act, the estate tax rates from before 2004 will go back into effect. That could boost the estate tax as high as 60 percent for estates between $10 million and $17,184,000.

Chapter **11**

GIVING WHILE YOU'RE ALIVE—ESTATE TRANSFER DURING LIFETIME

Many people enjoy giving away part of their estate while they are still alive so they can watch their family enjoy the gifts. This chapter explores what you must consider when you transfer your assets while you are still alive.

Question 146. **What is an inter vivos transfer (lifetime gift)?**

An inter vivos transfer includes any transfer of property between people who are still living. For example, if you give someone your home while you are still living without retaining rights to that home, you are making an inter vivos transfer. This gift would no longer be part of your estate at your death, because you no longer own it. To be counted as an inter vivos transfer, a gift must:

- Be given voluntarily to another person
- Be gratuitous, which means you can't have gotten anything in return
- Be accepted by the person who received the gift

Question 147. **What is a testamentary transfer?**

A testamentary transfer is the transfer of property or other assets through the use of a will after your death. The property or assets remain in your possession throughout your lifetime.

Question 148. **What are the advantages of an inter vivos transfer?**

Inter vivos transfers can be a valuable estate-planning tool that lets you give property away while you are alive and can watch the recipients enjoy the gift. It also gets the property out of your estate, which makes the probate process cheaper and easier. You may be able to save taxes. Here are the advantages:

- You can take advantage of the annual exclusion from gift and estate taxes of $12,000 per person or $24,000 per couple. This exclusion is not cumulative, and you can take it every year.
- The value of the gift is based on the year given, so you won't have additional taxes based on any appreciation in value that might impact the property between when you give it to the recipient and the time of your death. If you wait until your death, all that additional value can be taxed.
- If the gift involves the generation of a taxable income, by transferring the asset to a lower tax bracket recipient, you can reduce income taxes that must be paid on the taxable income generated.
- You don't have to pay any transfer tax on gifts out of pocket until your cumulative total of gifts exceeds the applicable

credit amount, which is $2 million in 2007 and 2008 and $3.5 million in 2009. In 2010 the estate tax is repealed, so you don't have to worry about any transfer in that year, but the estate tax will go back to its pre-2004 state if Congress doesn't act by 2011.

■ The transfer is not as public as a testamentary transfer, which must be filed with the court as part of probate.

■ If done properly, you can protect the assets from claims by creditors.

Question 149. **What are the disadvantages of an inter vivos transfer?**

You will find some disadvantages to an inter vivos transfer. The primary one is that the transfer cannot be revoked, so you cannot ever get the property back. You lose all control over it. Other disadvantages include:

■ You may need to pay gift taxes out of pocket if you exceed the annual exclusion.

■ If property values decline, you won't be able to reduce tax liability.

■ Sometimes tax law changes, and it would have been more beneficial to give the gift at a later date.

■ You lose control of the property and its income.

Question 150. **What are the consequences of an outright lifetime gift?**

When doing your estate planning, consider the following consequences of an outright lifetime gift:

■ You lose control over the asset.

■ You may have to pay gift taxes if the value of the gift exceeds the maximum gift tax annual exclusion.

- The asset is removed from your gross estate, but its taxable portion will be used when calculating the estate taxes as an adjusted taxable gift. (Read Chapter 6 for more information on this point).
- The donee will be responsible for any taxes for capital gains from the time he or she receives the asset until the time it is sold.
- The donee will need to report any income generated from the gift and pay taxes on it.
- The gifted asset will be taxed as part of the donee's estate if still owned, or the donee could have to pay gift taxes on the asset if he or she gives the asset away before death.

Question 151. What is an outright total interest charitable gift?

You make an outright gift when you give total interest in an asset to a charitable organization and get a charitable gift tax deduction, as well as a limited charitable income tax deduction. The charity must be on the list of qualified charities published by the IRS, and it must be in the form of cash or property. To qualify as an outright total interest charitable gift, you must give fee-simple title to the cash or property.

Question 152. What is a charitable bargain sale?

You can sell an asset to charity for less than its market value on the date of the sale and then take a charitable gift tax deduction for the difference between the sale price and the fair market value of the asset less the annual exclusion. This is called a charitable bargain sale.

Question 153. **What is a charitable stock bailout?**

A charitable stock bailout involves the donation to charity of a closely held stock. The donor gets a charitable gift tax deduction for the fair market value of the stock less the annual exclusion. In most cases, the stock will be redeemed by the privately held corporation for cash, since the charity wants the cash, and the remaining stockholders in this closely held company probably don't want a charity as a co-owner.

You cannot make a formal or informal agreement that the corporation will redeem the stock in order for this to qualify as a charitable stock bailout. In most cases a person chooses to use a charitable stock bailout to avoid paying capital gains that would be due if the stock were sold. The remaining shareholders increase their percentage of ownership by redeeming the shares.

Question 154. **What is a charitable gift annuity?**

A charitable gift annuity is a gift to a charity of a set amount per year during your lifetime. The actuarial value of this gift will be less than a cash donation or an outright donation of property because the gift will be given over a number of years. To calculate the charitable deduction for a charitable gift annuity, you would need to figure out the difference between the annuity and an outright cash gift and then subtract that difference less an annual exclusion.

The donor can name himself as the annuitant or he can name his spouse, and he won't have to pay any tax on the present value of the annuity. If he names his spouse, any interest given to her would qualify for a marital deduction. If anyone other than the donor or the spouse is named, the present value of the annuity is subject to gift tax. The donor can keep a portion of the gifted annuity as income, so this type of annuity is similar to a charitable remainder trust (see Question 115), but the advantage of using this type of annuity is that you don't have to go through the expense of setting up a trust.

Question 155. What is an outright partial interest charitable gift?

You can get a charitable gift tax deduction even if you only give a qualified charity a partial interest in your personal residence or farm. A personal residence can include any interest in real property, such as a vacation home or time-share, as long as the property is used as at least a part-time residence. Interestingly, even the remainder interest in a yacht can qualify, as long as it is used as a part-time residence. A farm is defined as any land used by the donor for the production of crops, fruit, or other agricultural products or for the care and feeding of livestock.

You can take the charitable gift tax deduction even if the charity's only interest is that it gets to take possession of the property involved after the donor's death or the death of someone named to have a life estate. For example, a husband can donate property and give his wife the right to life on the property until her death. After her death, the property would go to the charity.

Question 156. What is an intrafamily loan?

Anytime you make a loan to a family member at no interest or at an interest rate below the applicable federal rate as set by the IRS, the person who makes the loan is considered to have made a gift to the person who gets the loan. The amount of the interest that is not collected is considered as income to the person who made the loan even if though he doesn't get any cash. The uncollected cash, known as "imputed interest," is subject to gift tax.

You don't have to worry about imputed interest if the loan is less than $10,000 and is used to purchase non-income-producing property. You also don't have to worry about loans up to $100,000 for the purposes of buying business property as long as the borrower's net investment income is less than $1,000. Any imputed interest on this business loan is limited to the net investment interest income over $1,000. The borrower can deduct actual interest paid but cannot deduct the imputed interest amount.

Question 157. **What is a gift leaseback?**

A gift leaseback involves the giving of property in a fee-simple transfer to a closely held business owned or controlled by the donor. The donor then leases the property back from the business. Here are some reasons people enter into a gift leaseback:

- The business can deduct from taxes any lease payments, as long as the property involved is necessary for the operation of that business and the lease payments are reasonable for the type of property involved.
- The donor will be subject to gift tax on the fair market value of the gifted property less any annual exclusion at the time of the gift. If the property increases in value, the additional value will not be subject to gift tax.
- The gift property is removed from the donor's gross estate.

Question 158. **What is a reverse gift?**

A reverse gift can be a dangerous game played to eliminate taxable appreciation in property. The donor gives appreciated property to a donee who is expected to die before the donor. The donor gives the property with the idea that the donee will bequeath the property back to the donor as part of his or her estate, but this agreement cannot be in writing, and the donee cannot have a legal obligation to give back the property. So, you can give property with the idea that it will be a reverse gift and never get it back. The donee can decide to give the property to someone else, and you won't have a legal leg to stand on.

The reason people take this risk is that when the property is given back by the donee at death, the donor gets the property at the fair market value at the time of the donee's death, which means he avoids paying any capital gains on the property during the time the donee had the property, and it essentially eliminates the taxable appreciation of the asset. For this to work, the donee must have held the property for more than one year after receiving it before his or her death. If less than one year elapses before the donor gets the property back, the donor takes the decedent's adjusted basis immediately before death. The donee will have to include the value of the property in his or her gross estate.

Question 159. **What is a net gift?**

What do you do if you want to give property to your children but lack the cash you need to pay the gift tax? You can make a net gift, which means your child agrees to pay the gift tax, and the value of the gift is then reduced by the amount of tax your child pays. A net gift does not have to be to your child. It can be to any donee who agrees to the terms of the gift.

Another common type of net gift is a gift of property that still has a mortgage on it. The net gift would be the value of the property after subtracting the debt obligation. If the obligation that is assumed by the donee exceeds the donor's adjusted basis in the property, then the donor will have to recognize a capital gain on any excess value. The donor's estate can claim any gift tax paid out of pocket by the donee as a credit against the donor's estate tax even though the donee paid the tax. A net gift is similar to selling an asset at less than fair market value to a family member.

Question 160. **What is a custodial gift?**

If you don't want to go through the cost of setting up and maintaining a trust, but you do want to have some control of the assets, a custodial gift can be an excellent alternative. Custodial gifts are simple to set up and don't involve the payment of many fees.

You can administer the property or you can name a third party, such as a bank representative, to administer the gift. Custodial gifts are not a true trust because the minor beneficiary has both legal and equitable title to the property, but custodial gifts can function in a similar way to irrevocable trusts. The primary reason you save money on this type of gift is that trust documents don't have to be drawn up and executed. In fact, no document is necessary because the property is administered according to laws set up in each state under the Uniform Gifts to Minors Act.

Question 161. What is the Uniform Gifts to Minors Act?

Each state has its own version of the Uniform Gifts to Minors Act (UGMA) or the Uniform Transfers to Minors Act (UTMA). Many states started with the UGMA but switched to the UTMA. Here are the differences:

- The UGMA allowed gifts of only cash, securities, and life insurance, but the UTMA does not restrict the type of property you can give.
- The UGMA allowed you to make lifetime transfers only, but the UTMA allows you to make transfer to the trust during your lifetime as well as part of your will.
- The custodian of a UTMA has greater investment and management powers than the custodian of a UGMA.

In order to contribute to a UGMA or UTMA, you simply title the asset in the name of a competent adult who will serve as the custodian for the benefit of the minor beneficiary based on the statutes of your state. You must set up a separate UGMA or UTMA account for each minor. Often the donor will name himself or herself as the custodian.

Question 162. What are the elements of a gift in trust?

A more complex way to leave money to a minor or other person is to leave it as a gift in trust. A trust has five elements:

1. The person granting the trust must be legally and mentally competent. State law defines legal and mental competency, so

it has different meanings in each state. The person granting the trust can be called a grantor, settlor, or trustor.

2. The trustee, the person who manages the trust, must be legally and mentally competent as defined by state law. The trustee holds a legal interest in all trust property.

3. The beneficiary (there can be more than one beneficiary) holds an equitable or beneficial interest in the property. The beneficiaries can be classified as income or remainder beneficiaries. The income beneficiaries enjoy current income from the trust. The remainder beneficiaries get all assets left over when the trust ends. Most trusts are set up with a set limit to their term.

4. The property given to the trust is called the trust corpus or principal. In most situations, the grantor contributes most of the property in the trust, but property can be contributed by others. In some states, the trust corpus is titled in the trustee's name; in other states, the corpus is held in the name of the trustee acting in a fiduciary capacity.

5. The trustee has a fiduciary relationship with the beneficiaries of the trust. The trustee's fiduciary responsibilities include investment of the assets and managing the trust property in the best interests of the trust beneficiaries. He or she also has the responsibility to distribute the assets according to the terms of the trust.

Question 163. What are the goals of a trust?

Trustors set up a trust with numerous goals in mind, including the following:

- To allow the trust assets to benefit numerous beneficiaries at the same time. The trust can be set up so that some people get income during their lifetimes while others get the corpus of the trust when the term ends.
- Professional management of the funds, which can be particularly important if the beneficiary of the trust is a minor

child or a mentally incompetent adult. Also, professional management can be useful if the beneficiaries are not experienced with investing money or managing property.

- Avoiding probate by funding the trust while still alive.
- Protecting assets from the grantor's creditors, as long as the trust is set up as an irrevocable trust. If the assets in an irrevocable trust are set up with a spendthrift provision, they can be protected from the beneficiaries' creditors as well.
- Saving gift taxes by splitting the income among more than one beneficiary. You can also qualify for multiple annual exclusions and valuation discounts. You also reduce estate tax by eliminating assets from your gross estate (you can only eliminate taxes if you set up an irrevocable trust with no retained interest).

Question 164. **What is a minor's trust?**

A minor's trust is used when you want to give property to a minor but want the property to be administered by someone else until that minor is mature enough to handle the responsibilities of managing that property. You also probably don't want the trust to make mandatory income payments to the minor child. So a minor's trust is usually set up with income distribution at the discretion of the trustee, which means the minor will not have a present interest in the trust, and the grantor will not be able to take advantage of annual gift tax exclusions. You can set up the trust giving the minor present interest, but then the minor may have access to large sums of money earlier than you would like.

Question 165. **What are qualified tuition plans?**

A popular way to set aside money for your children are qualified tuition plans, also known as 529 plans because they were established by Section 529 of the IRS code. These plans are set up for the benefit of any person, including minors, provided there is an approved

sponsor. Approved sponsors include both private and public entities. Account balances grow tax free, and there is no required age
for distribution. You can also change the beneficiary of the account.
For example, suppose you set up a 529 for your child, but your child
decides not to go to college. You can then change the named beneficiary to another child, such as a niece, nephew, or grandchild.

You'll find two types of 529 plans on the market. Some are set
up by specific educational institutions, and you purchase prepaid
tuition credits; these are also called prepaid plans. Other types of
529 plans invest in mutual funds. In most cases, you are better off
selecting a type of plan that invests in mutual funds rather than one
that is tied to a specific educational institution.

You can contribute up to $12,000 per year per person into a
529 plan, and the gift will qualify for a gift tax exclusion, just like
other gifts. But 529s have a special provision that allows you to
contribute up to $60,000 in one year because the contributions can
be taxed as though they were made over a five-year period. Thus
all of this single contribution could qualify for five years of annual
exclusions and be completely exempt from the gift tax.

Question 166. What are Coverdell Education Savings Accounts?

Another type of educational savings account is the Coverdell ESA,
which is a trust or custodial account created solely for the purpose of paying qualified education expenses of the designated beneficiary of the account. When the account is first established, the
designated beneficiary must be under age eighteen or have special
needs. You must establish the account specifically as a Coverdell
ESA when you first open it. The conditions for setting up the
account include:

- The account must be set up with a trustee or custodian that
  is a bank or other entity approved by the IRS. Contributions
  must be in cash and must be made before the beneficiary
  reaches age eighteen unless the beneficiary is a special-

needs beneficiary. You cannot contribute more than $2,000 per year. You cannot invest the money in the account in life insurance contracts. You cannot combine the money in the account with other property except in a common trust fund or common investment fund. The account balance must be distributed within thirty days after the beneficiary reaches age thirty, unless the beneficiary is a special-needs beneficiary, or the beneficiary's death, whichever comes first.

You can set up a Coverdell ESA even if you already have a Section 529 plan in place. Funds in a Coverdell ESA grow tax free but can only be used for qualified educational expenses including tuition and fees, books, supplies, equipment, and academic tutoring. The maximum amount you can contribute to a Coverdell ESA is $2,000 per year.

Question 167. **What is a support trust?**

If you have the obligation to support someone else, you may decide either by choice or by court mandate to set up an irrevocable support trust. For example, in a divorce situation, the non-custodial parent can be required to fund an irrevocable trust with enough assets to guarantee that the child support payments will be made. Another common use of this kind of trust would be to provide long-term support for an incapacitated person.

Professionals who work in a field where their assets could potentially be seized by judgment creditors also may use an irrevocable support trust to protect those assets. For example, a doctor who could be sued for malpractice may use this kind of trust to protect his assets. The trust must be irrevocable to provide a shield from creditors.

With a support trust, the trustee has discretion over the distribution of both the principal and income for health, education, maintenance, and support of the beneficiary. To protect the trust assets from claims of the beneficiary's creditors, a spendthrift provision must be added to the trust.

When you establish a support trust, it may be subject to gift tax in the year it is established, but you won't be able to take an annual exclusion because the distributions of the trust are at the discretion of the trustee. Any income distributed to the beneficiary would be taxed, and the trust would pay tax on any accumulated income not given to the beneficiary.

Question 168. **What is a revocable trust?**

A revocable trust is one established during your lifetime and, as the name implies, is revocable, which means you can amend its terms during your lifetime. This type of trust provides no tax benefit and does not protect the assets from creditors, so its only purposes include:

- Avoiding probate by placing assets in a will substitute
- Providing a mechanism to handle the grantor's affairs in case the grantor becomes incompetent or incapacitated
- Providing a mechanism for a pour-over trust (see Question 171) after the grantor's death

You don't have to worry about gift taxes upon funding the trust; since you retain the right to revoke the trust, it is not a completed gift.

Question 169. **What is a contingent (standby) trust?**

This type of revocable trust is set up to establish a mechanism for your funds to be handled if you become incompetent or need to be away from home for an extended period. The primary difference in establishing a contingent trust is that you fund the trust with very little money at the time it is created. Instead of fully funding the trust initially, you attach a durable power of attorney to the trust, which gives someone the authority to transfer your assets into the trust if the named contingency happens. Often the person who has the power of attorney will also be the person named as the trustee.

For example, suppose you establish this trust when you are well, but you know that at some point your illness (such as Alzheimer's) will result in your being unable to handle your affairs. You would set up the trust and include a power of attorney. The power of attorney must specify how to determine whether you meet the contingency, which in this example would be competency. Sometimes the test of whether you met the contingency will be at the sole discretion of the named trustee, but often it will be by the concurrence of one or more physicians.

In addition to establishing the contingency and how the timing of the contingency will be determined, also name beneficiaries for any assets remaining in the trust after your death. You should include the right to revoke the trust so you can avoid the payment of any gift tax.

Question 170. **What are distributional trusts?**

While every type of trust has as one of its goals the proper administration and distribution of the trust's assets, several types of trust make this their primary purpose. The two most common types of distribution trusts are pour-over trusts (see Question 171) and dynasty trusts (see Question 172). Unlike other types of trusts, these trusts don't have other goals to meet, such as a contingent trust, which provides support after a person becomes unable to handle his or her affairs, or a support trust (see Question 169), which is set up to provide support for someone (see Question 167)

Question 171. **What is a pour-over trust?**

A pour-over trust is established during your lifetime as a place to put all your assets in one pot and then distribute them to multiple beneficiaries. It gets its name because assets are "poured" into the trust from numerous sources such as your will, life insurance proceeds, pension or profit-sharing plans, and other assets.

By establishing this type of trust, you can avoid probate (except for assets that are put into the trust after your death). A pour-over trust can avoid a second probate for assets that are left over because they were not distributed based on the terms of your will. Otherwise any remaining assets at the end of probate would need to go through a second probate to determine what to do with them. In many cases, a pour-over trust is a revocable living trust that continues after your death.

Question 172. **What is a dynasty trust?**

A dynasty trust is a type of trust that you can use to pass your assets to several generations of beneficiaries. Since any transfer to people who are two or more generations younger than you can be subject to the generation-skipping transfer tax (GSTT—see Chapter 10), this type of trust can be used to minimize that tax by taking advantage of the GSTT exemption. If set up properly, the trust can use the exemption to prevent the payment of GSTT each time it passes from one generation to the next.

To avoid the GSTT, you must create an irrevocable dynasty trust for the benefit of your descendants and fund the trust with property that you have allocated to all or part of your GSTT exemption. By doing this, the property will be subject to gift taxes only.

Most states put a time limit on dynasty trusts, but some states allow these funds to transfer in perpetuity. The states that let you set up perpetual trusts include Alaska, Arizona, Delaware, Idaho, Illinois, Maryland, South Dakota, and Wisconsin. Other states allow such a long lifespan that the trusts can almost be considered perpetual. For example, Wyoming allows you to establish a trust for 1,000 years, and Florida permits trusts to be established for 360 years. You don't have to live in a state to establish a trust there, so if you do want to establish a trust, be sure to do so in a state that meets your long-range plans.

Other advantages of the dynasty trust include:

- Protection of the assets from lawsuits during the descendant's lifetime, as long as properly drafted spendthrift provisions are added to the trust documents, which will limit the amount of money that can be taken out in any one year.
- Administrative and tax savings during probate.
- Prevention of the assets becoming marital property of the descendant so they cannot be subject to claims by a beneficiary's spouse in divorce.

Question 173. What is a mandatory income trust?

If you want to provide income annually to beneficiaries and take advantage of the gift tax annual exclusion, you can set up a mandatory income trust. This type of trust can be funded while you are alive or after your death. To qualify for the annual gift tax exclusions, however, you must fund it while you are alive.

You can set up the trust naming multiple income beneficiaries, and you can use the annual gift tax exclusion for each beneficiary, which was $12,000 in 2007. (The exclusion is adjusted by the IRS annually for inflation, if necessary, in multiples of $1,000.) The income beneficiaries have a present interest in the trust, and annual income must be paid out each year.

In addition to income beneficiaries, you can also name remainder beneficiaries who will get any principal left in the trust when the trust ends. There is no mandatory time at which this type of trust must end, but state law will limit the trust from being established in perpetuity unless the trust is set up in a state that allows perpetual trusts. Those states are Alaska, Arizona, Delaware, Idaho, Illinois, Maryland, South Dakota, and Wisconsin. As with dynasty trusts, some states allow these trusts to be set up with such a long lifespan as to make them, in effect, perpetual. You don't have to live in a state to establish a trust there, so be sure you choose a state that meets your long-range plans.

Question 174. **What is a Crummey trust?**

A Crummey trust is a way to take advantage of the annual gift tax exclusion by giving your child money each year but not actually giving the child the cash. For lifetime gifts to be eligible for the annual gift tax exclusion, the child must have a present interest; however, the Crummey trust allows you to control that interest. The trust is named for the Crummey family who took the IRS to court to win the right to restrict their children from taking money out of the trust at too young an age.

This type of trust gives your child the right to withdraw a gift thirty days after the gift is made. While she is younger, you don't have to worry. The trust meets the gift tax law by giving her a present interest, but she won't be old enough to even know she can take it. As she gets older, if she decides to withdraw an annual gift, you can stop making annual gifts to the trust.

After the thirty-day window for withdrawal, she cannot access the funds until the age that you set for distribution. This can be whatever age you set up in the trust. Commonly families will arrange for distributions at several different ages.

Crummey trusts provide more control over the money for a longer period than a custodial gift (see Questions 160 and 161), such as the Uniform Transfers to Minors Act. This allows children all access to the money at the age of twenty-one, and some states permit access as young as eighteen.

Question 175. **What is a grantor-retained annuity trust?**

You can set up a trust with provisions for you to receive an annuity amount from the trust at least annually by establishing a grantor-retained annuity trust (GRAT). Usually this annuity is set up based on a fixed percentage of the initial value of the trust assets. The payment of the trust can increase each year, but not by more than 120 percent of the previous year's amount.

This is an irrevocable trust funded while you are still alive. Usually these trusts are set up for a specific time, and in most cases, the grantor to the trust intends to outlive the terms of the trust. When the trust ends, its assets are distributed to the remaining beneficiaries. If the grantor dies before the term of the trust ends, any remaining funds in trust are included in the grantor's gross estate.

The present value of the remainder interest in the trust may be subject to gift tax. Compute the fair market value of the retained annuity interest; then deduct the value from the total trust assets to determine the amount of assets subject to the gift tax.

Question 176. **What is a grantor-retained unitrust?**

A grantor-retained unitrust, is similar to a GRAT (see Question 175) with one twist. The amount to be received as an annual annuity is based on a fixed percentage of the net fair market value of the trust assets as valued annually. The amount to be paid out can be greater than the annuity amount or trust amount. The amount to be paid will vary each year based on the value of the trust assets. This type of trust can provide better protection for the assets; if the fair market value drops dramatically because of a change in the underlying assets (such as a drop in the stock market), the annuity will be reduced to avoid using up the assets too quickly.

The present value of the remainder interest in the trust may be subject to gift tax. Compute the fair market value of the retained annuity interest using different tables than the GRAT to allow for the unitrust twist. Then deduct the value from the total trust assets to determine the amount of assets subject to the gift tax.

Question 177. **What is a grantor-retained interest (or income) trust?**

A grantor-retained interest or income trust provides the greatest protection for the trust corpus because the annual annuity from the trust is based solely on the income produced by the trust. If the income goes down, then the annuity goes down. If no income is generated in a particular year, no annuity will be paid from the trust. This trust will be subject to the highest gift tax and is seldom used in estate planning.

Question 178. **What is a qualified personal residence trust?**

If you want to stay in your house but set up a trust to gift the assets while you are still alive, you can set up a qualified personal residence trust (QPRT). You will retain the right to live in the personal residence for the term of the trust. Your present value in the trust will be your right to use the residence.

Determine any gift taxes by multiplying an income factor determined by the IRS times the fair market value of the residence. Subtract this income portion of the value from the full value of the assets at the time of funding to determine the portion of the value that will be subject to gift taxes.

Chapter **12**

SELLING PROPERTY—INTRAFAMILY TRANSFERS

Often family members will decide to sell property to each other at a price considerably below the market or with a series of installment payments. Whenever property transfers among family members, the IRS might take a look. This focuses on the key points to consider when selling property to family.

Question 179. What is an ordinary sale?

An ordinary sale between family members transfers property from one family member to another at the fair market value of the property. The seller gets payment for the full property value, and there is no gift to be considered. The property will no longer be part of the seller's gross estate, but any proceeds from the sale that are not used by his or her death will become part of the gross estate.

The family member who purchased the assets will need to report any income from the property bought. The seller will have to pay any capital gains tax that may be due on the property.

Question 180. **What is a bargain sale?**

This is when you sell property to a family member for less than its fair market value. The difference between the fair market value and the price you sold the property for could be subject to gift tax. You will be able to claim the annual gift tax exclusion of $12,000, or $24,000 if both you and your spouse sold the property together. Read more about the rules of the federal gift tax in Chapter 9.

Question 181. **What is an installment sale?**

Sometimes a family member will sell property to another family member, but the purchaser will not have to pay the full amount due in the year of the sale. Instead the purchaser will make payments over a number of years—thus, an installment sale.

If you enter into an installment sale, execute a promissory note to protect yourself. This note should state the number of payments as well as any interest rate to be paid. A big advantage of an installment sale is that you can recognize any gain from the sale over the number of years the installments are to be paid rather than recognizing all the gain in the year of the sale. Any gain is taxed as capital gains, and any interest paid on the loan is taxed as current income. If the interest is below current market prices, the difference in interest to be paid could be subject to gift taxes.

Question 182. **What are self-canceling installment notes?**

You can get set up an installment sale with a self-canceling installment note, which includes a provision that the purchaser's obligation to pay the note is canceled at the seller's death. The term on the note cannot exceed the expected life expectancy of the seller or the transaction will be taxed as a private annuity (see Question 183) rather than as an installment sale. If such a cancellation takes place, the seller's final federal tax form must recognize any gain that may occur with this change. As long as the note was drafted properly with the proper life span considered, the estate does not have to include the value of the canceled payments when calculating the gross estate. The purchaser of the property can deduct any interest paid as long as the property purchased is a business, residence or investment property.

This type of note allows the transfer of wealth prior to death without having to pay a transfer tax, if the seller dies early based on the actuarial mortality date. The seller can receive cash payments while still alive and still give the property to the person he had intended after his death without having to worry about gift or estate taxes on the property.

Question 183. **What are private annuities?**

Another way to structure an installment sale is as a private annuity. Instead of paying any unpaid amounts as installments, the amount of the payments due can be determined by one or more person's lifetimes. For example, if a son buys the residence of his parents, he can set up private annuity payments based on the expected lifespan of both parents.

The amount of the payments will be determined by dividing the fair market value of the property by the annuity factors shown in the government actuarial table. The son only needs to make these payments while the parents are still alive, so when they die, the private annuity can transfer wealth tax-free.

Don't worry about gift tax if the actuarially determined present value of the payments is equal to the fair market value of the property sold. The value of the property sold does not have to be included in the seller's gross estate.

Question 184. **What is a sales-leaseback transaction?**

You can sell business-related property to another and then lease that property back from the purchaser. This arrangement is called a sales-leaseback transaction. The buyer can either pay you in full for the property, or you can set up an installment arrangement for the payments.

If the asset was a capital asset, you will have to recognize a gain or loss on the transaction. The business that leases the property can write off the lease payments as long as they are reasonable and the property is necessary to the operation of the business. The buyer must report as income any lease payments made to her, and she likely will be able to depreciate the property.

Don't worry about gift taxes as long as the sale price equals the fair market value of the property. If the sales price is less than the fair market value, the difference in value between the sale price and the fair market value may be subject to gift taxes. You will have to include any unconsumed assets from this sale in your gross estate, but you will not have to include the property or its future appreciation in your gross estate.

Question 185. **What are remainder interest transactions?**

A remainder interest transaction involves assets you want to continue to use for the rest of your life, but you also want to get some cash benefit from the asset while you are still alive. You can do that by selling a remainder interest in the asset. The buyer will not be able to use the asset until you die, but he or she will get the asset eventually.

You will get some needed funds immediately, while the buyer gets the right to buy the property for an amount lower than the current fair market value. The purchase price is discounted because you can continue to use the property during your lifetime.

You must report all income from the asset until your death or until the life interest is sold. The asset will avoid probate at your death but will need to be included in the calculation of the gross estate. If the asset was not income producing, you will have converted the asset into an income-producing one by selling the remainder interest.

Question 186. **What are split interest transactions?**

The split interest transaction is similar to the remainder interest transaction (see Question 185), but each party buys his or her interest in the property at the same time. One party pays for the present value of the remainder interest while the other party pays for the present value of the income.

The IRS views this transaction as though the life interest holder in the split purchases the entire asset, and the value of the asset should be included in the gross estate. If the entire value of the asset is not included in the gross estate, the IRS will likely rule that the portion not included is a taxable gift and subject to gift taxes.

Chapter **13**

BUSINESS DEALINGS— TRANSFER OF CLOSELY HELD BUSINESS INTERESTS

Transferring a business among family members or partners can create a tax nightmare because businesses can have a sizable value for transfer tax purposes. There are a number of things to consider when making an intrafamily transfer of a closely held business. This chapter reviews the key issues involved in transferring business assets to a member of the family.

Question 187. What are buy-sell agreements?

One of the best ways to deal with the issues surrounding the transfer of a closely held business is to set up a buy-sell agreement at the time the business is formed. This type of agreement can take one of two forms:

1. *Cross-purchase agreement.* The business partners set up a contract to purchase the business from each other under specified circumstances, such as death, total disability, or retirement.
2. *Entity-purchase agreement.* Each business owner contracts with the business rather than with each other. The business entity has the obligation to purchase the person's share under specified circumstances, such as death, total disability, or retirement.

Whichever agreement exists, the key is that a mechanism will be in place for valuing the business. For example, a formula could be agreed upon that combines the book value of the assets as well as the good will established over the years of running the business. Also the process for buying the partner out of the business will be established.

Even if you have a buy-sell agreement in place, review the agreement and the process for buying out a partner. You want to be certain that the agreement reflects current family situations, as well as current market conditions. If you need to revise it, it's much easier to do when there isn't the stress that might arise if one of the specific circumstances come to pass.

Question 188. **What are restrictions upon transfer?**

Many times a closely held business will put restrictions on the transfer of any stock. These restrictions will give the remaining shareholders the right to buy the shares if one of the partners wants to sell before those shares can be offered to a third party not currently an owner in the company.

While restrictions upon transfer offer some protection to the shareholders, they do not guarantee that a problem won't arise when one of the partners wants to sell his or her shares and get out of the business. These restrictions usually do not establish a purchase price or a mechanism for setting one. Also, they do not establish a process for arranging what could be a sizable purchase for the remaining stockholders.

Question 189. **How do you transfer the business to a family member?**

To transfer your business a family member, you may need to make some changes to its structure before you transfer it, especially if you don't want to gift or sell the entire business at one time. First, you'll need to change the structure if your business is a sole proprietorship to form a business that allows multiple owners. This new form can be a partnership, a limited liability company, or a corporation.

Once the new structure is in place, you can then gift or sell interests in the partnership or shares of stock in the corporation. If you want to continue to control the business even though you gift or sell part of it to one or more family members, you will need to hold on to a majority of the shares that have voting power in making company decisions.

Question 190. **What are the gift tax implications?**

If you decide to give away a portion of your business as a gift to a family member, your gift may be subject to gift taxes. You value the transfer of corporate or partnership interests by subtracting the value of the interest you retain from the value of the interests held by all family members prior to the transfer. In most cases the retained interests are valued as zero if:

- Immediately before the transfer, you and any applicable family members hold control of the entity and retain a distribution right that does not have the right to receive qualified payments. Qualified payments are payments that are fixed in time and amount. Applicable family member includes one's spouse, any ancestor of either you or your spouse, and the spouse of any ancestor.
- You and your applicable family members retain a liquidation, put, call, or conversion right.

If your retained interests are valued at zero by the IRS, then your gift taxes will be much higher.

Question 191. **What are the estate tax implications?**

When calculating estate taxes after one's death, the original owner of the business can only include in his gross estate the business interest that he still holds at the time of his death. If the transfer of the business to other family members that took place during the decedent's lifetime resulted in taxable gifts, then the taxable gifts will become adjusted taxable gifts when the owner's estate tax is calculated.

Question 192. **What are the income tax implications?**

You won't have to worry about any income tax implications if you gift the business rather than sell it to family members. As long as your interests in the business were gifted, you do not have to recognize any capital gains.

What happens instead is that there will be a carryover basis from the owner to the donee family members. Both the original business owner and the donee family members will have to report income that can be attributed to their individual shares in the company.

Question 193. **What are the non-tax implications?**

You must also consider the non-tax implications of making a transfer of part of your business assets to a family member. The good news is that now you have family member donees who will take more of an interest in the operation of the business, if for no other reason than to protect their income.

You can prepare the family members who become involved in the business to take over when you retire or die. Family members who were gifted a portion of the business may be more interested in purchasing your shares at some point in the future. You may then want to set up a buy-sell agreement to arrange for the transfer of any remaining assets. A gift of a portion of your business may now make it a salable asset, whereas before you might have had trouble finding a buyer.

The bad news is that if your donee family members disagree with how you run the business, you may end up with a lot of arguments that you didn't have before. But as long as you hold the majority ownership, you will stay in control.

Chapter 14

LIFE INSURANCE PLANNING

Life insurance can and should become an integral part of your estate planning. Many families with closely held businesses use life insurance proceeds to pay any gift or estate taxes due upon transfer of the business so they won't be forced to sell the business when one of the owners dies. This chapter reviews various types of life insurance policies and the terms that drive them.

Question 194. What are important reasons to use life insurance as an estate-planning tool?

One of the first things a financial planner will do when beginning to work on your estate plan is to review your life insurance policies. Life insurance policies are critical to your estate plan for a number of reasons.

- *Estate liquidity.* All estates, whether large or small, need cash to pay any taxes, administrative costs, and debts left by the decedent. If there is a closely held business, cash is also needed to keep the business operating during probate and to pay an allowance to surviving family members during the time the estate is being administered. Life insurance proceeds can quickly fill this cash gap.
- *Retirement of debt.* The loss of the paycheck or Social Security check that used to come to the deceased person can be devastating to a family's budget. Major debts such as the mortgage of the home can be retired using a life insurance policy so the family will not be forced to move out of their home.
- *Replacement of income.* Life insurance policy proceeds can be used to fund an income stream for your family after your death.
- *Wealth accumulation.* You can use life insurance as a means to increase your family's wealth after the death of a family member.

Question 195. What is a joint-life policy?

A joint-life insurance policy covers more than one life. For example, sometimes business partners will buy a joint-life policy and specify that the face value of the policy will be paid to the surviving owner. In this case, the surviving owner would likely use the funds to buy out the family members of the partner who died. Another type of provision may specify that the face value of the insurance will be paid to certain beneficiaries after both people covered by the policy die.

Question 196. What is a first-to-die policy?

A first-to-die policy can be used in either a personal or a business situation. The policy terms specify that the face amount of the policy will be paid out upon the death of the first of one or more covered persons. When used in a business situation, the life insurance proceeds will likely be used to fund a buy-sell agreement (see Question 187).

A married couple will sometimes use this type of policy rather than fund two policies to cover each of their lives separately. The face value is paid out to the surviving spouse when one spouse dies. Life insurance proceeds at the death of the first spouse can be used to pay off a mortgage, fund children's education, replace the lost income of the person who died, or pay any estate taxes due.

Premiums on first-to-die life insurance are usually higher than the premiums would be if only one person were covered, but lower than the cost of carrying two or more individual life insurance policies.

Question 197. **What is a second-to-die policy?**

A second-to-die or survivorship policy is used by couples. It doesn't pay anything when the first person dies but instead pays the face value of the insurance at the time the last person who is covered dies. A married couple who wants to take full advantage of the unlimited marital deduction on their assets will frequently use a second-to-die policy to fund the payment of estate taxes.

Premiums for a second-to-die policy are lower than the cost of two separate policies. This type of policy might also make sense if one party is substantially older or rated higher because of illness or other factors. With this type of policy, underwriting will focus primarily on the status of the person who is likely to die last.

Question 198. **What are settlement options?**

After a person dies, the ways in which money is paid out to the beneficiaries are called settlement options. The owner of an insurance policy can specify how he or she wants the proceeds to be paid out or he or she can leave that decision up to the beneficiaries.

In most cases, life insurance death benefits are paid to beneficiaries in a lump sum, in installments, or in an interest-only option. Usually life insurance benefits received in a lump sum are tax-free to the recipient. If the owner of the policy or the beneficiary decides that the money will be paid in installments, any interest received on money not paid out immediately will be subject to income tax.

If an insurance policy owner specifies that the beneficiary should only be paid the interest generated by the insurance company on the death proceeds, and the death proceeds are paid out at a future date, then the total amount of the interest-only payments will be taxable income to the beneficiary.

Question 199. What types of ownership can you have in a life insurance policy?

The ownership of an insurance policy can have great gift and estate tax consequences. Here is a list of the possible types of ownership:

- Right to name and change the beneficiary
- Right to cash in, surrender, or cancel a policy
- Right to receive policy dividends
- Right to borrow against the cash values of the policy
- Right to pledge the policy as collateral for a loan
- Right to assign any of the foregoing rights or the policy itself
- Right to revoke any assignment of the rights

If a person dies with even one of these rights to any life insurance policy on the life of another person, the replacement value of that policy must be included in the owner's gross estate. But if the owner, insured, and decedent are all the same person, the death benefit is included in calculation of the gross estate. If the owner transferred his ownership to the life insurance policy to someone else during the last three years of his life, the death benefit also would be included in the gross estate.

Question 200. **What is a beneficiary designation?**

All life insurance policies permit the owner to designate who will get the death benefits of the policy. This person or persons are the beneficiaries, and the beneficiary designation permits you to name these people when you buy the policy.

When deciding whom to name as a beneficiary or beneficiaries on a life insurance, first consider how this policy fits into your estate plan and how it will help you meet the goals of that plan. If the primary purpose of buying that policy was to help cover any costs after your death, don't name someone who is not concerned with how the estate taxes or administrative costs of probate will be paid.

Question 201. **What is group term life insurance?**

When you get life insurance through work, the policy likely is a group term life insurance policy. This is a common fringe benefit in the workplace. An employer commonly establishes a face value to the term life policy that is usually equal to one year's salary or a set dollar amount.

A group term life insurance policy is owned by the employer. Your only right to ownership is the right to name a beneficiary or beneficiaries. In some cases, you will be allowed to convert the policy to an individual policy if you leave.

Any premiums the employer pays can be deducted as a business expense. The cost of coverage for the first $50,000 of life insurance benefits is not taxable income for the employee, even if they are paid by the employer. The cost for any coverage paid by the employer for a death benefit in excess of $50,000 is taxable income to employees. For example, if an employer pays for life insurance coverage up to $50,000, all premiums are nontaxable. But if the employer pays for a life insurance policy that gives someone $55,000 coverage, the difference of the cost between the $50,000 premium and the $55,000 premium would be taxable. That difference in premium would be added to the employee's income for the year and taxed at current tax rates.

The death benefit from a group term life insurance policy will be included when calculating the gross estate of the decedent, as long as the decedent had the right to name the beneficiary. The death benefit will not be included in the decedent's gross estate if the ownership of the policy was given to someone else more than three years before his or her death, but the gift of policy ownership may be subject to gift tax.

Question 202. **What is split-dollar life insurance?**

In a split-dollar life insurance policy, an employer and employee sign a written agreement that specifies how they will share the cost of a life insurance policy, as well as how the proceeds of the policy will be shared when the policy is surrendered either at the death of the employee or the termination of the employment. These types of policies are usually offered only to extremely valuable employees.

In most cases, the premiums paid toward increasing the cash surrender value of the policy are paid by the employer, while the employee pays the portion of the policy that buys the death benefit. Generally these agreements specify that the employer will receive any cash surrender value of the policy and the employee's beneficiaries will receive the death benefit.

Either the employee or employer can be the owner of the split-dollar life insurance policy. If the policy is owned by the employee, the employer secures her interest in the proceeds by having the employee sign a collateral assignment of the policy to the employer. If the policy is owned by the employer, she endorses the policy to allow the employee to designate the beneficiary of the portion of the life insurance proceeds granted to the employee under the agreement.

Question 203. **What is key person life insurance?**

Businesses purchase key person life insurance on the life of an employee who is key to the success of the business. The primary reason for this insurance is to replace the anticipated loss of income generated after the death of the key employee. In many cases, the insured employee is also an owner of the closely held business that purchased the life insurance.

Many closely held small businesses will use this type of life insurance policy to fund a buy-sell agreement (see Question 187). When the insured person dies, the proceeds of the life insurance policy are used to finance the buyout of the decedent's stock. The money is then used to pay any estate taxes, funeral expenses, and administrative expenses. The proceeds from a key person life insurance policy do not have to be included in the estate of the insured so long as no part of the proceeds are payable to a personal beneficiary.

Question 204. **What is a salary increase or selective pension plan?**

A salary increase or selective pension plan is a type of executive bonus plan used to supplement the compensation of highly paid employees for whom the maximum contribution to a qualified pension plan has already been made. The employer pays the entire premium on the employee's life insurance policy. The employee owns the policy and can name the beneficiaries. Since the owner of the policy is the employee, the proceeds paid at death must be included in the decedent's estate unless he assigns his right of ownership to someone else more than three years before his death.

Chapter **15**

ESTATE SHRINKAGE

Your estate likely will not be the same size at the time of your death as it will be when the final distribution of the estate is made—the value probably will be less. This shrinkage in value is caused by a number of factors, which I'll discuss in this chapter.

Question 205. **What causes an estate to shrink in size?**

Estate shrinkage is caused by a number of factors: administrative expenses to settle the estate, estate taxes, the payoff of any debts or claims by creditors, miscellaneous cash needs during the period of administration (see Question 206), and cash bequests (see Question 207). You can minimize estate shrinkage with property liquidity planning (see Questions 208 and 209).

Another cause of shrinkage can be litigation, if family members decide to challenge your will or any of its provisions. There are a number of ways to avoid litigation (see Question 210) and reduce attorney fees (see Question 211).

Question 206. **What are the miscellaneous cash needs of an estate?**

Miscellaneous cash needs of an estate vary widely. The estate may need cash to pay the family members an allowance or to keep a business operating during the period of estate administration. Proper planning can avoid draining the estate with these cash needs. For example, you can plan for a family allowance through buying a life insurance policy and using the cash from the death benefit to support the family until the estate can be settled, or you can set aside other cash assets in a will substitute that will not be subject to probate and the delays of settling the estate. Any cash needs of a small family-owned business can be covered using the proceeds of a key person life insurance policy (see Question 203).

Question 207. **What are cash bequests?**

A cash bequest is any provision in a will that gives a specific beneficiary a stated sum of money. You may be able to convince the beneficiary of a cash bequest to disclaim (give up) the cash or agree to accept the bequest through a distribution of property of equivalent value. This could eliminate the need and expense of converting non-cash estate assets into cash to pay the bequest.

If you must sell assets to cash to settle an estate, rarely will you get the full value of these assets because the sale becomes a forced liquidation. A forced liquidation is usually done as an auction, and the property goes to the person who makes the highest bid. Bidders, of course, will seek to pay the least amount possible, and most go to auctions looking for a bargain. The personal representative, who just wants to complete the job of administering the estate, likely will not want to wait until he or she can get a better price for the assets that must be sold.

Question 208. **What is estate liquidity planning?**

Liquidity planning is the process of figuring out the current and future cash needs of an estate and making sure you can meet these requirements from the assets that are in the probate estate to be controlled by your personal representative. You can also meet the cash needs of an estate using nonprobate assets that are passed to estate beneficiaries, but be sure those beneficiaries have a stake in meeting the cash needs of the probate process. For example, proceeds from a life insurance policy can be used to meet the cash needs of an estate.

If you do name a life insurance beneficiary who has no interest in the assets to be distributed by the estate, he or she may not feel the obligation to help pay estate expenses. Beneficiaries who expect to get assets from the estate will be more likely to help pay any taxes and other estate expense to avoid the forced liquidation of non-cash assets, because forced liquidation will likely result in sale of the assets at an amount below fair market value to get needed cash as quickly as possible. Another incentive for estate beneficiaries to help pay estate taxes is that the IRS can pursue beneficiaries to collect taxes due and can even put a lien against any property that was received from the decedent.

Question 209. **How can you reduce the cash needs of an estate?**

The best way is to use will substitutes and avoid any administrative expenses related to those assets, provided you can meet your estate's goal using these substitutes. Probate will be more expensive than any of the will substitutes you can use, but will substitutes won't always meet your needs. For example, you can place real-estate property in joint tenancy with right of survivorship (see Questions 41 and 42) to avoid the costs of probate, but you lose total control over the asset.

Every estate will have some assets over which the decedent wanted total control; these assets will need to go through probate.

You can reduce the estate's cash needs by minimizing the assets that will need to go through probate. That's because both the personal representative's fees and the attorney's fees will likely be based on the total of the assets that need to go through probate.

You can also minimize cash needs by reducing the number of hard assets, such as real estate or closely held business assets, whose value can be more difficult to determine than publicly traded stock. (Chapters 12 and 13 focus on ways to transfer these types of assets while you are still alive.)

Another way to reduce cash needs is to reduce any assets that may be difficult to manage in probate, such as rental property. If the personal representative has to spend more time managing certain assets, his or her fees will be higher.

Question 210. What causes an estate to become involved in litigation, and how can you avoid it?

The last thing you want to happen is for your estate to be tied up for years in litigation and for the assets you intended to go to your beneficiaries to end up paying legal fees. There are a number of strategies you can use to minimize the risk that your estate will be involved in litigation:

- Be sure that your will is executed based on the legal formalities of your state. Using a self-proving clause, when it's allowed by your state, will reduce any courtroom time and fees.
- If you plan to disinherit someone, expect them to contest your will. State the specific reason for disinheritance to prevent a successful will contest.
- If you loan money to someone and the estate needs to force collection of that debt, your estate may be involved in litigation. Avoid this situation by not making the loan; otherwise, the best protection is to carefully appraise the creditworthiness of the borrower.

- Your estate can end up in litigation if a creditor tries to collect on a debt from the estate and neither the creditor nor the decedent has proof of what is owed. Be sure all your debt agreements are in writing and keep careful records of repayments of those debts.

Question 211. How can you reduce attorney fees?

The best way is to minimize the size of your gross estate that must go through probate. In some states, attorneys can base their fees in part on the size of the estate, so the smaller an estate the lower the fees. Another good way to reduce attorney fees to is consider any possible holdings or actions that could result in litigation and take care of the questions while you are still alive. For example, if you plan to disinherit someone, amending your will to explain the reason will likely avoid a will contest after your death. If you owe someone money, be sure the debt is stated in writing and keep careful records of how much you paid, so your estate doesn't have to hire an attorney to defend against a claim from the creditor. If someone owes you money, be sure to make all attempts to collect that money before your death, so your estate doesn't have to pay an attorney to file a lawsuit for collection.

Question 212. How can you reduce estate taxes?

The best way is to reduce the size of your gross estate. You don't have to worry about taxes at all if your estate is less than $2 million in 2007 and 2008 or less than $3.5 million in 2009. You won't have to worry about estate taxes at all if you die in 2010. But, if you die in 2011 or after, what the estate taxes will be depends upon what Congress does. If Congress does nothing, start worrying about estate taxes if your estate is more than $1 million.

Given all the uncertainty about what estate taxes will be, your best bet is to minimize even the possibility that estate taxes will need to be paid by minimizing the size of your estate. You can do this in a number of ways including:

- Transfer incidents of ownership in your life insurance policy more than three years before your death. If you don't transfer ownership, the death benefit is included in your gross estate.
- If you plan to make major gifts upon which you will need to pay gift taxes, complete the gifts more than three years before your death. Any gift taxes paid within three years of your death will be included in the gross estate.
- If you retain a right to property that you have given away, give up that right more than three years before your death. Any property in which you have retained rights must be included in your gross estate.

Chapter **16**

POSTMORTEM
LIQUIDITY PLANNING

After you die, the possibility for increasing estate liquidity narrows considerably. That's because your personal representative must carry out the provisions of your will precisely without considering the effect of those provisions on liquidity. Yet there are some things a personal representative or family members can do to minimize the use of cash and maximize the amount of your assets that will be distributed to your beneficiaries. This chapter presents the postmortem actions that can be taken to minimize the use of cash before the estate is distributed.

Question 213. What actions can the personal representative take to maximize cash assets?

Your personal representative's attempts to maximize cash assets are limited to those assets that are under her control. Her first duty is to collect all probate assets. Liquid assets initially are the most important because she will be able to use those to pay any administrative expenses, debt obligations, or taxes. Liquid assets include:

- Any income that is received by the decedent after his death such as a final paycheck, royalties, commissions, and retirement benefits. Some retirement benefits that have named beneficiaries are not payable to the estate.
- Enforcement of a buy-sell agreement in which the surviving parties to the agreement pay out the cash promised by contract for the decedent's share of the business.
- Collection of death benefits from life insurance companies or employee benefits that are payable to the estate and not to named beneficiaries.
- Collection of any bank accounts, money market funds, or any other cash equivalents that do not go to a named beneficiary.

If the cash available to the estate is not enough to pay the expenses, debt obligations, or taxes, then your personal representative may have to make arrangements for a loan or to sell some of the non-cash assets.

Question 214. **What actions can the personal representative take to minimize cash needs?**

A personal representative can minimize cash needs primarily through strategies concerning the payment of three taxes: the federal estate tax, the federal income tax, and the federal generation-skipping transfer tax. To minimize the federal tax, he must first consider the value of the assets and whether to set that value at the date of the decedent's death or six months later. The best date to choose will be the one that results in the lowest tax bill. He can also minimize federal estate tax payments by being certain he takes advantage of all possible deductions (see Chapter 6). Finally, he can minimize the cash needs for taxes by being certain that he pays the taxes on time to avoid any penalties and interest.

Question 215. What are qualified disclaimers, and how do they aid in postmortem planning?

A qualified disclaimer occurs when a beneficiary refuses the bequest of property from a decedent. To find out what makes a disclaimer qualified or defective, see Question 129. A qualified disclaimer aids postmortem liquidity planning because the personal representative does not have to worry about paying the cash specified in the bequest. If a beneficiary other than the spouse refuses a bequest, the value of the bequest will go to the spouse and be qualified for the unlimited marital deduction, so no estate taxes will need to be paid on the asset. A surviving spouse can disclaim a marital deduction bequest to avoid wasting the available estate tax applicable credit amount. This will lower the surviving spouse's estate tax obligations.

Question 216. What is a spousal elective share?

If the spouse is not happy with the share of the estate she was given and she lives in a common law state, she can elect against the will and take a statutory percentage of the estate rather than the amount given in the will. This decision is known as the spousal elective share. She must file a notice with the personal representative that she intends to exercise her rights under the statute. See Question 12 for more information about common law states.

This decision can dramatically impact the other beneficiaries as well as the liquidity of the estate because if the spouse elects to take more than specified in the will, other beneficiaries will get less. The only advantage to the other beneficiaries is that this election will reduce estate taxes because the spouse's share will qualify for the unlimited marital deduction. The reduced tax bill will free up more cash for the other beneficiaries.

Question 217. **What are homestead, exempt property, and family allowances?**

Most states protect the surviving spouse and dependent children from the probate laws through three state laws: homestead, exempt property, and family allowances. The homestead and exempt property allowances give the family rights to certain property to protect beneficiaries from being left penniless. The family allowance law mandates that the family must be paid a certain amount from the estate during the period of estate administration.

Family allowance laws can impact the liquidity of the estate because in most states they must be paid in cash. Homestead and exempt property allowances can be satisfied by distributions in kind, such as giving the family home to the family to satisfy the homestead requirement.

In most states, the surviving spouse and children must elect to claim these allowances by notifying the personal representative in writing.

Question 218. **Why would a will be contested?**

A decedent can leave his property to anyone he wants through a will as long as he meets these three assumptions when the will is executed:

1. He is legally and mentally competent to make a will.
2. He executes a valid will.
3. He expresses his wishes in the will in a clear and understandable matter.

If a person is not satisfied with what she receives in the will, she can contest the will in probate court. She can seek to have the court declare the will invalid because one of the three assumptions are not met, or she can ask the court to interpret something that is not clear in a way that is more beneficial to her.

If the will is declared invalid, the probate estate will be distributed based on the state's intestacy laws (see Chapter 4). Only a person who stands to gain more from a distribution by state law would contest a will to have it declared invalid.

Question 219. **What is a family settlement agreement?**

Sometimes to avoid the costs and delays of litigation, the family members involved will negotiate a settlement to avoid a will contest. This is called a family settlement agreement. To reach agreement, family members impacted by any settlement would have to convince all beneficiaries to agree to the compromise and avoid litigation. A family settlement agreement must get the approval of the probate judge before it can be enforced, but the judge will likely agree with the family provided the language in the will is subject to different interpretations.

Chapter 17

PROBLEMS OF INCOMPETENCY

Unfortunately, some people are faced with the possibility that they will not be competent to handle their affairs throughout their lifetime. Often people don't think about this possibility. When it actually happens, it can be too late for them to do anything about it. This chapter explores the problems that arise when someone becomes incompetent.

Question 220. **Who can be considered incompetent?**

People of any age can become unable to manage the basics of daily life and care for their property or financial affairs. A person can be considered incompetent if he or she lacks the ability or capacity to communicate responsible decisions concerning his or her personal life or financial affairs.

A minor child who has not reached the legal age of majority in the state in which she lives, which is twenty-one in most states and eighteen in other states, is considered incompetent. An adult with diminished capacity can also be considered incompetent. This can happen because of mental illness or deficiency, physical illness or disability, advanced age, chronic use of alcohol or drugs, confinement, detention by a foreign power, or disappearance.

Question 221. **Why don't people plan for incompetency?**

Most people don't expect to be incapacitated and have no idea of what problems it can cause. Others who may be aware of the possibility don't want to think about such an unpleasant situation. Others don't plan because they think they will have lasting health until it's their time to die. Probably the most common reason is procrastination.

Sometimes people understand the need to plan for the possibility of incompetency but decide they just don't like any of the preplanning techniques or don't want to pay any of the up-front costs, such as fees to a planner or attorney to execute the necessary documents. Others may decide not to preplan because they don't want to hurt the feelings of a family member or friend by choosing someone else to manage their affairs.

Question 222. **What are state-mandated court-ordered arrangements for people to handle the financial affairs of an incompetent person?**

When you don't plan for your incompetency, the state mandates a court-ordered arrangement. So exactly how your financial affairs will be handled if you become incompetent will depend upon the laws of the state in which you live. The state will appoint a guardian to take responsibility for both you and your property when you are declared incompetent (see Question 223 about guardianship).

Question 223. **What is guardianship, and how does it work?**

Guardianship involves any arrangement in which a person takes responsibility for the care of another person and his or her property. Court-ordered guardianship will provide for the care of an incompetent person. The guardian or guardians of an estate, when ordered by the court, will manage an incompetent person's financial affairs.

Plenary guardianship is a court-ordered arrangement that involves the complete control of an incompetent person and his or her property. It includes the person's daily activities, living arrangements, non-emergency health care, and any other necessary activities. In addition, it includes the management of the incompetent person's financial affairs, which results in the of his or her basic civil and property rights.

The person who is deemed incompetent becomes a ward of the state. The court-appointed guardian acts under and within the state's authority to protect the ward in a fiduciary capacity. Most states have a list of priorities for appointment of a guardian based on the relationship to the adult incompetent person. First will be a person who held the most recent durable power of attorney. Next will be a spouse or person designated in the incompetent person's will. Next will be an adult child, followed by any family member with whom the incapacitated person has lived in the past six months. The last choice will be a person nominated by the person who is caring for or paying for an incapacitated person's care.

Question 224. **What is conservatorship, and how does it work?**

A conservator is a court-appointed person who protects and manages the financial affairs of an incompetent person. A conservator can be appointed if the court finds that a person needs protection because she is unable to manage her property. In addition, the court must find that the property owned by the incompetent person might be wasted unless proper management is provided. A conservatorship can also be mandated if the court finds it is necessary or desirable to protect assets so there will be funds available for the person's support, care, and welfare.

Question 225. How do you establish a guardianship or conservatorship?

Any person who has an interest in a person's welfare can file an action with the court. In many cases, the person who files a court action will be a family member. Because the resulting court mandate could result in the person's loss of civil and property rights if he is declared incompetent, the person will be represented by a guardian ad litem (a person appointed by the court to protect his rights during the court proceedings). Lay and expert testimony will be presented to the court regarding why the person should be declared incompetent. If the court agrees with the person filing the action, it will appoint a guardian or conservator and will declare the person incompetent.

Question 226. What are the powers and limits of guardianship and conservatorship?

The state mandates specific powers to a guardian or conservator. The powers and limits to those powers include:

- A guardian for a minor has the powers and responsibilities similar to those of a parent. He will be responsible for the minor's support, care, and education but is not personally liable for the minor's expenses or liable for third-party acts of the minor.
- A guardian for an incapacitated person has any powers that are necessary or desirable so she can provide continuing care and supervision.

■ A conservator has the powers necessary to manage and distribute the incompetent person's property for her support, education, care, or other benefits the conservator deems desirable. The only power a conservator does not have over an incompetent person's finances is the power to make a will.

Question 227. **What are limited guardianships?**

Every power and duty given to a guardian deprives the incapacitated person of civil and property rights. This can include the right to control his or her living arrangements and daily activities. A limited guardianship imposes restrictions on the guardian's powers, allowing the person who has been declared incompetent to make some decisions himself. A limited guardianship encourages the maximum self-reliance and independence of the incapacitated person.

Question 228. **What are limited conservatorships?**

Like a guardianship, a conservatorship deprives the incompetent person of civil and property rights. This can include the right to write checks, the right to make gifts, and the right to contract with others. It can also include the right to buy and sell property and the right to sue and be sued. A limited conservatorship restricts the powers of the conservator to handling specific transactions or types of transactions as manager of specific areas of the incompetent's person's financial affairs.

Question 229. **What are the advantages of guardianships and conservatorships?**

The primary advantage of guardianships is that they provide for continuing care and supervision of a minor or incapacitated person's living arrangements and daily activities. The main advantage of conservatorships is that they protect and productively manage an incompetent person's property and other financial affairs. Other advantages are that the court has supervisory and enforcement powers to ensure a guardian or conservator is acting in a fiduciary capacity to protect the incompetent person according to the state's authority.

Question 230. What are the disadvantages of guardianships and conservatorships?

While you might like the idea of letting the courts make the tough decisions about incompetency so you don't have to plan for it, consider the disadvantages of court-ordered arrangements.

- They can be dehumanizing, since most states require that the person be declared mentally ill or incompetent before they will step in. This will require that evidence be presented to the court.
- They can be uncertain, time-consuming, and costly. Papers must be filed, expert testimony must be arranged and paid for, and if anyone challenges the incompetency, both sides must be represented in court.
- They can be inflexible in the powers granted. In most situations, the arrangements are not tailored to the specific situation.
- They may be uncertain regarding who will care for the person or manage the person's property. The person appointed may not be the one desired by the incapacitated person.

You are much better off making these decisions yourself by planning for incompetency while you are able to do so (see Chapter 18).

Chapter **18**

PLANNING FOR INCOMPETENCY

Chapter 17 presented the problems of not planning for your incompetency, which can leave you with little control over what you can do each day. This chapter focuses on how to plan for your incompetency. By spending a little time on planning and a bit of money on setting up the desired alternative, you can have a lot more control over what will happen to you if you become incapacitated or incompetent at some point.

Question 231. **How do you plan for the management of a non-minor's financial affairs?**

There are a number of alternatives to consider in planning for possible incapacity or incompetence. Some cost you nothing, others will involve minimal legal fees, and still others may involve the costs of setting up a trust. Your choices include:

- Establishing a joint convenience checking account (see Question 232)
- Executing a durable power of attorney (see Question 233)
- Funding a revocable living trust (see Question 234)
- Funding a contingent revocable living trust in combination with a durable power of attorney (see Question 235)
- Setting up a special needs trust (see Question 236)
- Drafting your own voluntary limited conservatorship (see Question 237)

Question 232. **What is a joint convenience checking account?**

A joint checking account is the simplest thing you can do to set up a mechanism for your finances to be handled by someone you choose. Simply follow the rules required by your bank to set up such an account. As long as your state laws authorize a joint convenience checking account, it's better to use those forms than an account with joint tenancy with right of survivor. With the convenience checking account, your cosigner is limited to withdrawing funds solely for the benefit of the incompetent or incapacitated person, while the cosigner of a joint tenancy account has the right to withdraw funds for any reason.

If a cosigner on a joint convenience checking account uses funds for himself, there could be gift tax implications for the incompetent person. If there is any income on a joint convenience checking account, the income will be taxed on the incompetent person's account.

Any money left in a joint convenience checking account after the incompetent person dies becomes part of the decedent's estate to be distributed based on the provisions in the will. Any money left in a joint tenancy account will go to the person who was the joint tenant and bypass probate.

Setting up a joint convenience checking account works best if these conditions exist:

- The funds you put into the account are needed for routine expenditures.
- You need assistance with a task of routine bill paying.
- You can handle cash for food and clothing purchases and other basic expenses, or you have a trusted person who can make these purchases for you.
- You have a trusted person in mind as cosigner who is willing to take on the responsibility of handling your bill paying.

Question 233. **What is a durable power of attorney?**

A durable power of attorney creates an agency relationship between one person (who is the principal) and another person or institution (who is the attorney-in-fact). The scope of the durable power of attorney can be very broad, giving the attorney-in-fact permission to do any act the principal can do except to execute a will, or it can be very limited. For example, the attorney-in-fact can be given only the right to perform one specific act, such as to sell a piece of property.

You can set up a durable power of attorney as long as you have the legal capacity to appoint someone else to perform an act for you. State law determines whether you have the legal capacity.

You can't use a traditional nondurable power of attorney for preplanning for incapacity because the powers of an attorney-in-fact cease when the principal is no longer legally competent to complete the act. In all fifty states, a durable power of attorney remains in effect even after the person is incompetent.

Question 234. **What is a funded revocable living trust?**

You can prepare for the possibility of becoming incapacitated and unable to handle your affairs by funding a revocable living trust. Usually the grantor of the trust is also the trustee. To fund the trust, title all appropriate property by making the revocable living trust the holder of legal title to the property. In most cases, the grantor (you) or the grantor and his or her spouse are sole lifetime benefi-ciaries of the trust. You will continue to manage the assets of the trust, as well as your own finances, in the same way you did in the past, but now as a trustee of the revocable living trust.

With all the legal work in place and the trust funded, the only action you need to take when planning for possible incapacity is to draw up (or have drawn up) a trust document specifying what will happen when and if you become incompetent or die.

When you become incompetent, you are removed as the trustee, and the full trust powers will go to a co-trustee or a suc-cessor trustee who was named while you still had the legal capacity to choose who you wanted to manage the trust. The trust allows the assets in the trust to avoid probate and may also provide for the management of the property after your death.

Since this will not be a completed gift because the trust is revocable, you don't have to worry about gift taxes. The total value of assets remaining in the trust when you die will be included in the calculation of the gross estate for estate tax purposes.

Question 235. **What is a contingent (standby) trust?**

You might like the idea of a revocable living trust as the means to manage your property and finances if you become incapacitated, but you don't want to fund that trust immediately. A good alterna-tive is to set up a contingent or standby trust with minimal funding (it can be as low as $5) as long as you execute a durable power of attorney. The person named in this durable power of attorney as your attorney-in-fact will take responsibility for fully funding the trust and naming the trustee should you become incapacitated.

The power you give the person named in the durable power of attorney can be either immediate or "springing." Springing means that the durable power of attorney will not take effect until you become incapacitated. You set up the terms of the trust agreement and specify the duties, powers, and discretion of the trustee, whom you can also name.

Should you become incapacitated, the attorney-in-fact changes the title of the principal's assets from the principal to the trustee. The trustee then manages the property based on the terms you set when you set up the trust.

Question 236. **What is a special needs / Craven trust?**

A special needs or Craven trust is an irrevocable trust set up for the benefit of someone else. Often this type of trust is set up by a parent for the care of a disabled child or by an adult child for the care of an elderly parent. The trustee usually is given discretionary power over the distribution of the income from the trust.

If the trust is created during the grantor's life, the trust income will be taxable either to the trust or to the income beneficiary because the trust is irrevocable.

If the grantor retains too much control over the trust distributions or if the trust distributions are used to pay a legal support obligation, then the trust income will be taxable to the grantor.

If the grantor relinquishes all control in the trust, the assets of the trust will not be included in his gross estate. But if the grantor retains too much control, the assets will be included in his or her gross estate. Creating and funding the trust during the grantor's lifetime could result in gift taxes.

Question 237. **What is voluntary, limited conservatorship?**

Chapter 17 discussed state-mandated conservatorships, but you can avoid this by setting up a voluntary, limited conservatorship for the management of your financial affairs should you become incompetent. Not all states authorize these types of conservatorships, but if your state does, you have the right to pick the conservator and control his or her powers. You can also more easily dissolve a voluntary, limited conservatorship than you can a state-mandated one.

This type of conservatorship is based on the fact that the conservator will only need to deal with part of your financial affairs.

For example, this type of conservatorship might be used if you can continue to handle routine, smaller expenditures but need help with large sums of money or major purchases.

The primary advantages are that you get to pick the person who will handle your finances, and you avoid the stigma of being found to be totally incompetent. You do still need to go before the court to establish the conservatorship.

Chapter 19

AN INCOMPETENT PERSON'S MEDICAL NEEDS

Another set of decisions that must be made for an incompetent person relate to medical care. You need to decide who will make medical decisions for you if you no longer have the capacity to do so. If you don't pick someone as part of your preplanning for incompetency, the state will get to make that choice.

Question 238. **What is informed consent?**

Each time you need medical treatment, you or someone else must give consent for that treatment. This type of consent is called informed consent. The Supreme Court has ruled that a person who is recognized as competent has the right to refuse unwanted medical treatment.

Each state has the right to set up appropriate procedures for informed consent. Some states recognize the right to refuse life-sustaining treatment, and others permit the right to withhold or withdraw treatment. Even if family members and a patient's physician disagree with a patient's choice to withhold or withdraw treatment, the patient's right to decide is key as long as the patient is considered capable of understanding the consequences of his or her decision.

Question 239. What is substituted judgment?

Sometimes a patient may no longer be capable of making decisions or communicating those decisions to his doctor, so he cannot give his informed consent to proposed medical treatments. When this happens, a family member, a friend, or someone else in the health-care system will need to make all medical decisions for the incompetent person. This type of situation can be handled in two ways:

1. If the patient's wishes are known and were conveyed to a family member or friend, the courts will usually respect the wishes of the incompetent person even if the wishes are not in writing.
2. If the patient's wishes are not known, the court uses the doctrine of substituted judgment. Under this rule, family members or others close to the person are authorized by the court to make medical decisions for the incapacitated patient because the courts have ruled that these people will best know the patient's feelings and value system.

If you don't preplan for incapacity, you will have no control over who can make medical decisions for you and your wishes will not be in writing. If you have specific feelings about when and if life-sustaining treatment should be withheld or withdrawn, put them in writing while you are still competent to do so.

Question 240. **What are living wills?**

If you want to be certain that your wishes about medical treatment are followed even if you become incompetent, put those wishes in writing, using a living will. This document will state your intentions and give specific directions concerning medical treatment at the end of life in the event you become terminally or incurably ill or injured and are incapable of granting or withholding consent for treatment.

The most common purpose of a living will is to state your wishes to be allowed to die without the application of life-prolonging measures you believe are futile. The living will can also be used to request certain types of treatment or pain relief, including artificial respiration or ventilation, heart pumping, dialysis, certain types of pain medications, and artificial feeding. The best type of living will specifies when you want these procedures done and when you want them withheld. For example, you may want these procedures withheld if you arc in a coma and if you are not expected to wake up.

States set the rules for when these provisions are honored and when they can be ignored. Some states consider the living will to be advisory and a guide to medical providers. Also, the medical provider is the one who decides if the patient's condition is terminal or meets other specified wishes of the patient in order for the provisions of the living will to be followed. If you have a living will, discuss the provisions that are important to you with your medical provider, so he or she will know what your wishes are.

Question 241. **Why designate another person to make medical decisions?**

In most states, the living will law applies only if an incompetent person's condition is terminal, so you still should designate another person to make medical decisions for you if you become incompetent but are not considered terminal. The person you designate can also make sure that your medical provider is following your wishes as specified in your living will. The person you designate can use his or her authority to either litigate to enforce your wishes as stated in your living will or to change medical providers. He or she will be able to make decisions on issues that are not covered in your living will because the courts will deem that person has knowledge of your wishes and values, as well as any specific instructions you may have given to your appointed agent.

You can appoint someone to make medical decisions for you if you become incompetent by completing a health-care proxy (see Question 242), by appointing a health-care agent under specialized state statutes (see Question 243), or by appointing an attorney-in-fact using a durable power of attorney for the purpose of making medical decisions (see Question 233).

Question 242. **What is a proxy appointment?**

In some states, one way to designate someone to make medical decisions for you if you should become incompetent is by proxy appointment. Your proxy appointment can be included in your living will. Other states require you to make a proxy appointment in a separate document.

Proxies can act only when you are in a condition specified in state statutes, which is usually when you are in a terminal condition as defined in the statute.

Question 243. **What is a medical power of attorney?**

Another way to provide for a health-care agent is to use a separate document called a durable power of attorney for health care or a document that meets the medical treatment decisions statute of your state. These types of documents allow a person to make health-care decisions for you, including a decision to withhold or withdraw life support.

You also can appoint an attorney-in-fact using a durable power of attorney (see Question 233). While this type of document is usually used in conjunction with the management of money or property, there is nothing in state statutes or court decisions that restricts the durable power of attorney in such matters. Some states require the use of a durable power of attorney for health care, so be sure to seek legal advice in your state.

A health-care agent or a medical attorney-in-fact appointed under the durable power of attorney can usually make decisions for an incapacitated person whether or not you are terminal. The powers granted to an attorney-in-fact for health-care decisions can be broad or limited. There are variations in each state regarding the amount of power that can be granted.

Question 244. **What is a medical decision-making agent?**

A medical decision-making agent is anyone you designate to make medical decisions for you using a medical power of attorney. A medical decision-making agent can also be a medical attorney-in-fact who was appointed using a durable power of attorney in most states. Some states will only accept your medical decision-making agent if a durable power of attorney for health care is in place.

In whatever document you decide to use to appoint your medical decision-making agent, specifically authorize your medical decision-making agent:

- To have access to your medical records and the ability to disclose these medical records to communicate your previous treatment decisions
- To have the power to interpret your living will
- To have the power to give, refuse, or withdraw consent for specific medical or surgical measures based on your condition, prognosis, and known wishes
- To employ, discharge, and grant releases to medical personnel
- To start legal action, if necessary, and to get authorization for specific treatment decisions
- To spend or withhold funds needed to carry out medical treatment

Question 245. **What are medical directives?**

A medical directive is any directive written in advance of becoming ill and pertains to treatment preferences. The medical directive will also designate a person who can make decisions for you in the event that you become unable to make those decisions on your own behalf. The three most common types of medical directives are living wills, power of attorneys, and health-care proxies.

Question 246. **What is a do not resuscitate order?**

A do not resuscitate order (DNR) is an order specifying that if the signatory's heart stops or if she stops breathing, no one should attempt to resuscitate her. As long as the patient is competent, she can sign this order and specify that it is in effect until she revokes it. Hospital procedures are in place to determine how to make DNR decisions, resolve disputes that may arise among medical personnel or family members, and protect the patient's right to refuse treatment in such emergency situations.

If a patient is incompetent and has no DNR order in place, then the decision is usually made after the medical providers have consulted with family members, friends, a legal guardian, or a court-appointed representative. A living will can play a crucial role in this decision if the patient refuses artificial life-sustaining procedures in that will under certain circumstances.

Chapter **20**

ESTATE PLANNING FOR COHABITATION OR NONTRADITIONAL FAMILY ARRANGEMENTS

People who decide to live together and not get married in the traditional sense must make different types of arrangement for estate planning because they cannot take advantage of many of the provisions in estate law that married couples have. This chapter reviews some key considerations in your estate planning if you live with someone or are involved in some other type of nontraditional family arrangement.

Question 247. What is a property agreement, and why do you need it?

If you have not married the person with whom you cohabitate, you should at the very least draft a property agreement that can be used to settle any disagreements over what should happen to property accumulated both before and after the relationship began. This type of agreement can help you avoid both an emotional and financially draining legal battle. Some points you should include in a property agreement include:

- *Responsibility for the debts.* Specify who will pay which debts. Without a specific agreement, a cohabitant will be responsible for any debts to which he or she cosigned or for any assets that are owned jointly. Loans that involve commingled income-producing assets will be the responsibility of the cohabitants who cosigned the loan.
- *Household contribution.* Specify in writing each cohabitant's household contribution and what it covers.
- *Division of assets.* Specify in writing a list of all assets in the household, who owns them, and whether any other cohabitant has a claim on each asset. Include the value of each asset and the dates they were acquired. In addition, title any assets that were acquired during the cohabitation relationship to reflect the desired ownership rights. You can title property as tenants in common, which means each tenant owns an equal share, or joint tenants with rights of survivorship, which means the asset will automatically go to the cohabitant who survives.
- *Residence.* Specify what happens to the residence if one of the cohabitants dies. If the property is to be sold when the cohabitation ends, the method of disposition should be in writing.
- *Children.* If children are part of the cohabitation arrangement, specify who will be responsible for their personal and financial care both during the relationship and after the relationship ends.
- *Termination.* Specify under what circumstances the agreement will be terminated. This can include separation, mutual consent, incompatibility, death or the marriage of one cohabitant to someone else, or other mutually agreed upon terms.

■ *Dispute settlement.* Include provisions for how a dispute can be settled other than by litigation, such as mediation or arbitration.

Question 248. How do you use a living revocable trust in nontraditional family arrangements?

One good tool for solving the problems that arise when you are doing estate planning for a nontraditional family is the living revocable trust. It allows cohabitants to place shared assets into a trust that can specify that property in the trust will pass to the surviving cohabitant. Since this trust is revocable, either cohabitant can change his or her mind and pull out his or her share of the assets.

This trust has a major advantage over a will because the property in the trust can pass to the surviving cohabitant without having to go through probate. The cohabitants may also be able to avoid a possible will contest from one of the deceased cohabitant's family members. During the grantor's lifetime, beneficiaries can be changed and the trust can be altered, amended, or abolished completely.

Question 249. What are estate tax strategies for nontraditional family arrangements?

Nontraditional families can't take advantage of some of the estate tax avoidance strategies offered to married couples, such as gift splitting (see Question 134), the gift tax marital deduction (see Question 95), or the estate tax marital deduction (see Question 59), so their strategies to avoid estate taxes can be very different.

While you can't save estate taxes by bequeathing your property to your cohabitant because the property will be part of your gross estate, it is really your only choice if you want to maintain control of the property throughout your lifetime. A lifetime gift to avoid estate taxes can be risky, however, because possession and control passes immediately to your cohabitant; if the relationship does deteriorate, you can't get it back.

The best way to lower the value of your gross estate to avoid estate taxes is a charitable bequest. For example, if the value of your estate is $2.3 million, which is $300,000 higher than the allowable exclusion amount ($2 million in 2007 and 2008), then you could leave $300,000 to charity and avoid all estate taxes.

Since you can't take advantage of the marital deductions, you may end up paying more in estate taxes. One way to fund the payment of those taxes is to buy a life insurance policy and name your cohabitant as the beneficiary. If the relationship deteriorates, you can always change the beneficiary of the policy.

Question 250. **What are the lifetime gift strategies for nontraditional family arrangements?**

You can take advantage of the annual gift tax exclusion and make gifts to your cohabitants during your lifetime. A gift of $12,000 or less in 2007 can be excluded from gift taxes. This exclusion can be taken every year and is not cumulative. The exclusion amount is adjusted periodically to the nearest $1,000. The primary disadvantage of gifting property is that you lose all control over that property for the rest of your life.

Another tactic that you can consider to be certain your cohabitant will be able to continue to use property after your death is to title the property as tenants in common. While this strategy won't avoid estate taxes, because the property is still retained by the donor, and may result in gift taxes, it lowers a person's gross estate. Only the portion held by each tenant in common will be included in a decedent's gross estate. For example, if you own property worth $150,000 and title it as tenants in common with your cohabitant, each of you would only need to add $75,000 to your gross estates.

THE 250 QUESTIONS

Chapter 1:
The Basics of Estate Planning

1. What is estate planning?

2. Who needs estate planning?

3. What are the financial goals of estate planning?

4. What are the non-financial goals of estate planning?

5. What are the tax goals of estate planning?

Chapter 2:
Taking Time for Probate

6. What is probate?

7. What property interests are affected by probate?

8. What are the objectives and process of probate?

9. Who is a personal representative, and what are his/her duties?

10. What is a will?

11. What is a community property state?

12. What is a common law state?

13. How do laws differ between a community property state and a common law state?

14. What happens if a child is omitted from the will?

15. What rights to adopted or illegitimate children have to an estate?

16. What are abatement statutes?

17. What are ademption statutes?

18. What are anti-lapse statutes?

19. What are divorce or annulment statutes?

20. What are simultaneous death statutes?

21. What are tax apportionment statutes?

22. In which state does probate occur?

23. What is the difference between residence and domicile in estate law?

24. What are the advantages of probate?

25. What are the disadvantages of probate?

Chapter 3:
When There's a Will

26. What are the requirements for a valid will?

27. What are the typical clauses of a will?

28. What are dispositive clauses of a will?

29. What are appointment clauses of a will?

30. What are concluding clauses of a will?

31. What is a no-contest clause in a will?

32. What are other common clauses in a will that are optional?

33. How do you amend or revoke a will?

Chapter 4:
Intestate—When There's Not a Will

34. What happens if you die without a will (intestate)?

35. In intestacy laws, what provisions are made for survivors?

36. What provisions can be made for charities or non-family members?

37. What provisions are made if there are no surviving family members?

38. How is the estate distributed if a person dies intestate?

39. What are the disadvantages of intestacy?

Chapter 5:
Will Substitutes or How to Avoid Probate

40. How can you avoid probate?

41. What are rights of survivorship?

42. What is joint tenancy?

43. What is a beneficiary?

44. How can a government savings bond be used as a will substitute?

45. How can POD accounts be used as a will substitute?

46. What are Totten trusts?

47. What are TOD accounts?

48. What are gifts causa mortis?

49. What are revocable living trusts?

50. What are irrevocable living trusts?

51. How can provisions in contracts be used to avoid a will?

52. What are the advantages of a will substitute?

53. What are the disadvantages of a will substitute?

Chapter 6:
Dealing with Taxes—Federal Unified Transfer Tax System

54. What is the federal unified transfer tax system?

55. What is a gift tax?

56. What is an estate tax?

57. What is a generation-skipping tax?

58. What is EGTRRA, and how does it impact the federal unified transfer tax system?

59. What is the marital deduction?

60. What is the charitable deduction?

61. What is the applicable credit (or unified credit)?

62. What is the fair market value of an estate?

63. How do you determine the fair market value of real estate?

64. How do you determine the fair market value of closely held stock?

65. How do you determine the value of life insurance?

66. How do you determine the fair market value of corporate stocks and bonds?

67. How do you determine the fair market value of annuities?

68. How do you determine the value of a U.S. government bond?

69. How do you determine the value of property held as a co-ownership?

70. How do you determine the value of property held as tenancy in common?

71. How do you determine the value of property held as joint tenancy with right of survival?

72. How do you determine the value of property held as tenancy by the entirety and community property?

73. What date is used for the valuation of property?

74. How do you report and pay federal estate tax?

Chapter 7:
Calculating the Estate Tax

75. What are the key parts of calculating estate tax?

76. What is the difference in calculating estate tax versus income tax?

77. What is the gross estate?

78. Which property is calculated in the gross estate?

79. Is life insurance part of the gross estate?

80. How is joint property calculated in the gross estate?

81. Are survivorship benefits (retirement benefits, pensions, annuities) included in the gross estate?

82. Is property subject to a qualified conservation easement included in the gross estate?

83. What are lifetime transfers, and how are they included in the gross estate?

84. If a person retains a lifetime interest in property, is that included in the gross estate?

85. What is retaining a reversionary interest and is it included in the gross estate?

86. What is retaining the rights to alter, terminate, revoke, or amend the transfer of property, and is the property included in the gross estate?

87. What is the three-year inclusionary rule?

88. What can be deducted from the gross estate?

89. How are debts, mortgages, and liens deducted from the gross estate?

90. How do you calculate funeral expenses to be deducted from the gross estate?

91. What administrative expenses can be deducted from the gross estate?

92. Can you deduct estate taxes paid to a foreign government?

93. What theft and casualty losses can be deducted from the gross estate?

94. What state estate taxes can be deducted from the gross estate?

95. What is the marital deduction, and how is it calculated?

96. How much can be deducted in charitable contributions from the gross estate?

97. What are adjusted taxable gifts, and how do they impact the calculation of the estate tax?

98. What is the gift taxes payable credit?

99. What is the applicable credit?

100. What is the credit for federal gift taxes?

101. What is the credit for foreign estate taxes?

102. What is the prior transfer credit?

Chapter 8:
Estate Tax Planning

103. What are the goals of estate tax planning?

104. How can you reduce the gross estate?

105. How can you preserve or increase the estate tax deductions and credits?

106. How do you manage the marital deduction for estate tax planning purposes?

107. What is the power of appointment trust (marital trust)?

108. What is an estate trust?

109. What is the QTIP Trust?

110. What is bypass planning?

111. What strategies can be used to combine marital and bypass trusts?

112. How do you use the charitable deduction in estate tax planning?

113. What is the remainder trust in a farm or personal residence?

114. What is a charitable lead trust?

115. What is a charitable remainder trust?

116. What are a charitable remainder annuity trust and a charitable remainder unitrust?

117. What are pooled income funds?

118. What is a qualified funeral trust?

Chapter 9:
Rules on Giving—Federal Gift Tax

119. What is a gift?

120. How do you calculate the fair market value of gifts?

121. What are the filing requirements for gifts?

122. What are special valuations for intrafamily transfers?

123. How is the valuation for purposes of gift taxes determined on lifetime transfers?

124. How is the valuation calculated on retained interests trusts and term interests?

125. What is the effect of buy-sell agreements, options, and restrictions on valuation on the gift tax?

126. How are lapsing rights or restrictions treated under gift tax rules?

127. What is a lifetime transfer, and when is it complete?

128. How does adding your child's name to property impact the gift tax?

129. What is a defective disclaimer?

130. What transfers of property are exempt from the gift tax?

131. What qualifies as an educational exemption?

132. What qualifies as a medical exemption?

133. How do you calculate total calendar-year gifts?

134. How can you split gifts with your spouse?

135. What is the annual exclusion?

136. What are gift tax deductions?

137. What qualifies for the marital deduction of gift taxes?

138. What qualifies for the charitable deduction of gift taxes?

Chapter 10:
Generation-Skipping Transfer Tax

139. What is the generation-skipping transfer tax?

140. What is the difference between a skip person and a non-skip person?

141. What is a direct skip?

142. What is an indirect skip?

143. What is the GSTT exemption?

144. How do you calculate the GSTT?

145. What is the applicable rate for the GSTT?

Chapter 11:
Giving While You're Alive—Estate Transfer During Lifetime

146. What is an inter vivos transfer (lifetime gift)?

147. What is a testamentary transfer?

148. What are the advantages of an inter vivos transfer?

149. What are the disadvantages of an inter vivos transfer?

150. What are the consequences of an outright lifetime gift?

151. What is an outright total interest charitable gift?

152. What is a charitable bargain sale?

153. What is a charitable stock bailout?

154. What is a charitable gift annuity?

155. What is an outright partial interest charitable gift?

156. What is an intrafamily loan?

157. What is a gift leaseback?

158. What is a reverse gift?

159. What is a net gift?

160. What is a custodial gift?

161. What is the Uniform Gifts to Minors Act?

162. What are the elements of a gift in trust?

163. What are the goals of a trust?

164. What is a minor's trust?

165. What are qualified tuition plans?

166. What are Coverdell Education Savings Accounts?

167. What is a support trust?

168. What is a revocable trust?

169. What is a contingent (standby) trust?

170. What are distributional trusts?

171. What is a pour-over trust?

172. What is a dynasty trust?

173. What is a mandatory income trust?

174. What is a Crummey trust?

175. What is a grantor-retained annuity trust?

176. What is a grantor-retained unitrust?

177. What is a grantor-retained interest (or income) trust?

178. What is a qualified personal residence trust?

Chapter 12:
Selling Property—Intrafamily Transfers

179. What is an ordinary sale?

180. What is a bargain sale?

181. What is an installment sale?

182. What are self-canceling installment notes?

183. What are private annuities?

184. What is a sales-leaseback transaction?

185. What are remainder interest transactions?

186. What are split interest transactions?

Chapter 13:
Business Dealings—Transfer of Closely Held Business Interests

187. What are buy-sell agreements?

188. What are restrictions upon transfer?

189. How do you transfer the business to a family member?

190. What are the gift tax implications?

191. What are the estate tax implications?

192. What are the income tax implications?

193. What are the non-tax implications?

Chapter 14:
Life Insurance Planning

194. What are important reasons to use life insurance as an estate-planning tool?

195. What is a joint-life policy?

196. What is a first-to-die policy?

197. What is a second-to-die policy?

198. What are settlement options?

199. What types of ownership can you have in a life insurance policy?

200. What is a beneficiary designation?

201. What is group term life insurance?

202. What is split-dollar life insurance?

203. What is key person life insurance?

204. What is a salary increase or selective pension plan?

Chapter 15:
Estate Shrinkage

205.What causes an estate to shrink in size?

206.What are the miscellaneous cash needs of an estate?

207. What are cash bequests?

208.What is estate liquidity planning?

209.How can you reduce the cash needs of an estate?

210.What causes an estate to become involved in litigation, and how can you avoid it?

211. How can you reduce attorney fees?

212.How can you reduce estate taxes?

Chapter 16:
Postmortem Liquidity Planning

213.What actions can the personal representative take to maximize cash assets?

214.What actions can the personal representative take to minimize cash needs?

215.What are qualified disclaimers, and how do they aid in postmortem planning?

216.What is a spousal elective share?

217. What are homestead, exempt property, and family allowances?

218.Why would a will be contested?

219.What is a family settlement agreement?

Chapter 17:
Problems of Incompetency

220.Who can be considered incompetent?

221. Why don't people plan for incompetency?

222.What are state-mandated court-ordered arrangements for people to handle the financial affairs of an incompetent person?

223.What is guardianship, and how does it work?

224.What is conservatorship, and how does it work?

225.How do I establish a guardianship or conservatorship?

226.What are the powers and limits of guardianship and conservatorship?

227. What are limited guardianships?

228.What are limited conservatorships?

229.What are the advantages of guardianships and conservatorships?

230.What are the disadvantages of guardianships and conservatorships?

Chapter 18:
Planning for Incompetency

231. How do you plan for the management of a non-minor's financial affairs?

232.What is a joint convenience checking account?

233.What is a durable power of attorney?

234.What is a funded revocable living trust?

235.What is a contingent (standby) trust?

236.What is a special needs / Craven trust?

237. What is voluntary, limited conservatorship?

Chapter 19:
An Incompetent Person's Medical Needs

238. What is informed consent?

239. What is substituted judgment?

240. What are living wills?

241. Why designate another person to make medical decisions?

242. What is a proxy appointment?

243. What is a medical power of attorney?

244. What is a medical decision-making agent?

245. What are medical directives?

246. What is a do not resuscitate order?

Chapter 20:
Estate Planning for Cohabitation or Nontraditional Family Arrangements

247. What is a property agreement, and why do you need it?

248. How do you use a living revocable trust in nontraditional family arrangements?

249. What are the estate tax strategies for nontraditional family arrangements?

250. What are the lifetime gift strategies for nontraditional family arrangements?

INDEX

About the Author

Lita Epstein, who earned her M.B.A. from Emory University's Goizueta Business School, enjoys helping people develop good financial, investing, and tax-planning skills. After completing her M.B.A. she managed finances for a small nonprofit organization and for the facilities management section of a large medical clinic.

She designs and teaches online courses on topics such as investing for retirement, getting ready for tax time, and finance and investing for women. She's written more than twenty books including *Working after Retirement for Dummies, Reading Financial Reports for Dummies, Trading for Dummies, Complete Idiot's Guide to Social Security and Medicare, Complete Idiot's Guide to Tax Breaks and Deductions,* and *The 250 Questions You Should Ask to Avoid Foreclosure.*

Lita was the content director for a financial services Web site, MostChoice.com, and managed the Web site Investing for Women. As a congressional press secretary, Lita gained firsthand knowledge about how to work within and around the federal bureaucracy, which gives her great insight into how government programs work. In the past, Lita has been a daily newspaper reporter, magazine editor, and fundraiser for the international activities of former President Jimmy Carter through The Carter Center.